C000072251

The Sugar Act and the American Revolution

Journal of the American Revolution Books highlight the latest research on new or lesser-known topics of the revolutionary era. The *Journal of the American Revolution* is an online resource and annual volume that provides educational, peer-reviewed articles by professional historians and experts in American Revolution studies.

Other Titles in the Series

1764: The First Year of the American Revolution
by Ken Shumate

Anatomy of a Massacre: The Destruction of Gnadenhutten, 1782
by Eric Sterner

The Burning of His Majesty's Schooner Gaspee:
An Attack on Crown Rule Before the American Revolution
by Steven Park

General Peter Muhlenberg: A Virginia Officer of the Continental Line
by Michael Cecere

Grand Forage 1778: The Battleground Around New York City
by Todd W. Braisted

The Invasion of Virginia 1781
by Michael Cecere

John Adams vs. Thomas Paine: Rival Plans for the New Republic
by Jett B. Connor

March to Independence:
The American Revolution in the Southern Colonies, 1775–1776
by Michael Cecere

The Road to Concord: How Four Stolen Cannon Ignited
the Revolutionary War
by J. L. Bell

Washington's War, 1779
by Benjamin Lee Huggins

A JOURNAL OF THE AMERICAN REVOLUTION BOOK

THE SUGAR ACT
AND THE
AMERICAN REVOLUTION

KEN SHUMATE

WESTHOLME
Yardley

Westholme Publishing, LLC
904 Edgewood Road
Yardley, Pennsylvania 19067
Visit our Web site at www.westholmepublishing.com

ISBN: 978-1-59416-396-8
Also available as an eBook.

Printed in the United States of America.

CONTENTS

Preface   *vii*

Introduction   *x*

Prologue   *xiii*

PART ONE: *Duties for Trade Regulation*

1. The Sugar Act of 1733   3

2. Revise and Enforce   17

3. Reasons Against the Renewal   29

PART TWO: *Duties for Trade Regulation and Revenue*

4. The Sugar Act of 1764   43

5. Protest   85

6. The British Retreat   98

PART THREE: *Duties for Revenue*

7. The Sugar Act of 1766   117

8. A Distinction Without a Difference   139

9. Demand for Repeal   151

Notes   163
Bibliography   183
Index   195

PREFACE

T HE STORY OF THE SUGAR ACT IS ONE OF THE LONGEST, MOST complex stories of the American Revolution. It begins before Great Britain in 1764 initiated parliamentary taxation of America, and ends in 1774 with Americans declaring that the Sugar Act infringed upon and violated the rights of the colonists. Along the way, it served as the vehicle for an overhaul of British colonial policy. There were three acts passed by Parliament—in 1733, 1764, and 1766—that established trade regulations and levied duties on products imported into the British North American colonies. Each act was, in its own time, called the Sugar Act. American protests to the Sugar Act duties and regulations laid the foundation for the persistent and often violent protests against the Stamp Act and the Townshend Acts. Understanding the long Sugar Act controversy provides insight into events of the decade of crises beginning in 1764.

The act of 1733 was the first dealing with America that used words of donation associated with revenue acts: giving and granting money to the king. Although it levied duties on imported foreign products—sugar, rum, and molasses—it was in fact a trade regulation. The duties and the duplicitous words of giving and granting were simply a façade to facilitate its passage in Parliament. For decades it had little effect on American commerce, never enforced during the long period of British "wise and salutary neglect" of the colonies. The end of such neglect in 1763—enforcement of the act—marked the beginning of a change in colonial policy.

The act of 1764 amended the act of 1733, including adding duties and specific words to its purpose: "it is just and necessary that a revenue be raised." It was also designed to regulate trade: "extending and securing the navigation and commerce between Great Britain and your Majesty's dominions in America." It levied import duties intended both to raise revenue and to regulate trade as preferential tariffs in favor of British products. The duties were dual-purpose, as was the act itself. That the duties were levied in order to raise revenue established the Sugar Act as the first act of Parliament to impose taxes on America. British statesman Edmund Burke made it starkly clear to the House of Commons in 1774. "No act avowedly for the purpose of revenue," he said, "is found in the statute book until . . . the year 1764. All before this period stood on commercial regulation and restraint." The Sugar Act "opened a new principle: and here properly began the second period of the policy of this country with regard to the colonies; by which the scheme of a regular plantation parliamentary revenue was adopted."[1] The colonies did not at first recognize it as an act of taxation, with few exceptions treating its duties as trade regulation, and protesting only the resulting adverse effect on commerce—particularly protesting the high duty on foreign molasses, a product essential to the economy of the northern colonies on the continent.

The act of 1766 amended the act of 1764, reducing the duty on foreign molasses to a low level acceptable to American merchants, while at the same time placing the same duty on imported British molasses. This action resolved the dual-purpose nature of the molasses duty, transforming it into a straightforward tax. The effect of the reduction in the rate of duty—Americans still not seeing the Sugar Act as taxation—was payment of the duties without protest, resulting in the exaction of more revenue from America than any other parliamentary taxation.

Eventually, additional British acts of taxation awoke Americans to a realization that the duties of the Sugar Act were taxation as well, and subversive of American rights. The First Continental Congress in 1774 demanded repeal of the Sugar Act as being "essentially necessary in order to restore harmony between Great Britain and the American colonies."[2]

INTRODUCTION

"What do We mean by the American Revolution? Do We mean the American War? The Revolution was effected before the War commenced. The Revolution was in the Minds and Hearts of the People."

—John Adams, 1818

THE SUGAR ACT PLACED CUSTOMS DUTIES ON PRODUCTS IMPORTED into the British colonies in North America, starting in 1733 with sugar, rum, and molasses from foreign colonies. In 1764, a revision to that act imposed additional duties, and in 1766 further revision resulted in—after almost another decade—Americans seeing the Sugar Act as the first act of Parliament to tax the colonies. The center of the story is the Sugar Act of 1764: in addition to taxation, it was the vehicle for an overhaul of British colonial policy. Historian Joseph Ellis has pointed out that following the Seven Years' War, "the first manifestation of a new imperial policy . . . was the Proclamation of 1763," while the next installment came "in the form of three acts of Parliament: the Sugar Act (1764), Stamp Act (1765), and Townshend Acts (1767)."[1]

As part of telling the story about that act of 1764, my plan is to first describe the act it amends (the Sugar Act of 1733) and end by describing the act (the Sugar Act of 1766) that, in turn, amends the act of 1764. Treating each as a separate entity, an incarnation of the Sugar Act, sets up the next aspect of my strategy: presenting the American reaction to each of the acts—reasons against renewal of the act of 1733, protests against the act of 1764, and a call for repeal of the entire Sugar Act.

An important part of the story is the detrimental effect of the Sugar Act on American commerce with foreign colonies in the West Indies as a consequence of duties levied on foreign sugar, rum, and—especially—molasses. Of the duties imposed in 1733, it was the molasses duty that brought forth the loudest American protest. Lowered in 1764, the molasses duty nevertheless continued to disrupt colonial commerce, again drawing strident protest. Finally, in 1766, the rate was reduced once again but levied in such a manner that it was transformed into an outright tax. Subsequently, despite being a tax, the molasses duty drew little protest from the Americans, and accounted for more revenue than duties placed on any other product imported into America. John Adams, in a reflective mood long after America and Great Britain went their separate ways, wrote this sentiment. "I know not why we should blush to confess that molasses was an essential ingredient in American independence."[2]

Beginning in 1767, the British imposed additional duties in the same form as those imposed by the Sugar Act. To British surprise, the Americans saw those duties as taxes—and protested. After a long period of reaction-counter-reaction (eventually involving the infamous tax on tea) the Americans rejected all parliamentary duties for the purpose of raising revenue. The First Continental Congress in 1774 made the blunt statement that several acts—first naming the Sugar Act—imposed "duties for the purpose of raising a revenue in America" and as a consequence were "subversive of American rights."[3]

I feature taxation both when describing the nature and effect of the Sugar Act, and when describing American protests. There is broad agreement on the primacy of taxation. According to historian Merrill Jensen, "It was direct parliamentary taxation of the colonies after 1763 that began the final dispute between Britain and the American colonies." And taxation led to this: "The overriding constitu-

tional issue of the age was the precise status of the colonial governments within the British Empire, and ultimately, the relationship between the British legislature and the colonial legislatures."[4]

I believe in the particular fitness of contemporary writing to tell
the story (despite odd and inconsistent spelling and punctuation). I
annotate extracts from statutes, petitions, letters, parliamentary debates, and other official documents, using the original text in order
to provide the essence of this eighteenth-century controversy. Presenting the original text not only preserves the meaning and emphasis
of the original words (enhanced, I hope, by my annotation), it allows
the flavor and style and subtle shades of meaning to shine through
as well. In order to hold this book to a reasonable length while telling
the story through many varied sources, I restrict coverage to those
aspects of the Sugar Act that best explain its role in the American
Revolution, and often provide only a small extract of even a lengthy
document.

My intent is to provide insight into the Sugar Act—why it was enacted in 1733, why and how it was modified in 1764 and 1766, and
how Americans reacted to each incarnation—in order to establish a
foundation for understanding the following decade in which British
colonial policy took a disastrous turn, eventually leading to war and
independence of the American colonies.

PROLOGUE

"No sugar, rum or melasses of the plantations of foreign nations shall be imported into Britain or Ireland, or to any of the King's dominions in America. . . . Whereas great numbers of horses and great quantities of lumber have been exported from our Continent colonies to the foreign sugar colonies, whereby they are enabled more easily to carry on their said sugar plantations, none such were to be transported hereafter to those foreign colonies."
—The Sugar Bill, 1731

IN THE EARLY EIGHTEENTH CENTURY, THE ECONOMY OF THE British colonies in North America was dependent on plentiful and inexpensive imported molasses, there distilled into rum for domestic consumption and as an export necessary to obtain specie for the purchase of manufactured goods from Great Britain. Americans in the northern continental colonies—New England and New York—imported molasses, sugar, and rum from sugar-producing islands in the West Indies (both British and foreign colonies), most often in exchange for fish, beef, lumber, horses, and other provisions necessary for the livelihood of the largely single-crop sugar plantations.

Plantation owners in the British colonies, in dire competition with foreign plantations for the European sugar market, resented that their sibling colonies provided the foreign colonies with these indispensable supplies, and complained to British officials that the trade should be prohibited. Americans maintained that the trade was necessary since the British plantations could not provide sufficient molasses to meet American needs, nor could the British islands take all the produce needed to be exported from the northern colonies. Eventually, the British sugar planters decided to appeal to the House of Commons to stop the trade between the Americans and the foreign sugar islands. They had reason to believe their appeal would be looked upon with favor, a number of members of the House of Commons having substantial financial interests in the West Indies.

Let's take a look at one insightful paper out of a blizzard of pamphlets and letters pro and con regarding this American trade. On October 3, 1730, the Board of Trade took up an essay supporting the British islands. "Mr. Dunbar, Surveyor General of H.M. Customs [for the West Indies] has drawn up a state of the English Sugar Colonys, with respect to the trade of the Northern Colonys." The essay argues that the foreign colonies benefit from trade with New England, obtaining provisions unavailable from any other source. The foreign sugar plantations could not

> subsist without the horses from New England, nor . . . without New England lumber, such as staves, hoops and beading especially, consequently [if they did not have such supplies] little sugar could be made among them, at least not in the vast quantitys that at present glutt the European marketts and render our own sugars vendible only in Great Britain and Ireland.

Furthermore, "the French and Dutch Settlements vend their melass which they would otherwise lose, for to still it into rum is not worth their while."[1] As a consequence, molasses ("melass" and many alternate spellings) was plentiful and cheap in the foreign islands. (One important factor was that France allowed no production of rum as it threatened the brandy trade.) Remedies proposed:

(i) that the *export* of horses, lumber and provisions from the Northern Colonys, to the Dutch and French Settlements [be prohibited];

That remedy solved the problem of foreign colonies obtaining the provisions they needed for prosperous plantations. Then,

[(i) continued] as well as the *importation* of melass and rum from thence into the said Colonys, [also be] prohibited.

That remedy put a halt to the foreign colonies being able to "vend their melass which they would otherwise lose."

Dunbar turned to sugar, and an imbalance in duties that discriminated against British exports. Enumerated goods exported to America from the British islands (goods listed in the Navigation Act of 1660) were subject to duty. The duties were levied in 1673 by 25 Charles II c.7, often called the Plantation Act. (Such duties were intended primarily for regulation of trade, and commonly referred to as plantation duties or enumerated duties.) Of interest to our story is the duty on sugar: "Sugar, White the hundred Weight containing one hundred and twelve pounds: five shillings;" and "Browne Sugar and Muscavadoes the hundred Weight . . . one shilling & six pence." (To a useful approximation, white sugar was at least partially refined, while brown sugar and muscovado sugars were more-or-less unrefined.) Dunbar proposes leveling the playing field, along the way, giving a name (one among various ambiguous names) to the two sides in what will be a long-standing controversy: "British sugar colonys" vs. "British Colonys in America," i.e., the continental colonies. (Although the British colonies in the West Indies were in "America," common, but inconsistent, terminology generally uses the words America and American to refer to the British colonies on the continent of North America, and not the islands.)

(ii) As there is no law that prohibits the importation of commoditys of the product of foreign settlements into our northern and southern colonys (when in free bottoms), *or which subjects them to the payment of any duty*, therefore as the product of the *British sugar colonys pay* . . . the enumerated duty, I humbly conceive

that dutys at least equivalent to those of our own, ought to be imposed on the product of the French and Dutch Settlements when
imported into our *British Colonys in America*, then trade would
be upon a more equal footing.[2]

British planters petitioned the House of Commons on February
23, 1731:

A Petition of several merchants, planters and others, trading to
and interested in his Majesty's Sugar Colonies in America [the islands in the West Indies], was presented to the House in behalf of
themselves and many others, complaining That divers of his
Majesty's subjects, residing within his dominions in America
[North America] . . . had of late years carried on a trade to the
foreign Sugar Colonies in America, from whence they were supplied with sugar, rum, molosses, and their other productions, instead of those from our own colonies.

It is worth immediate mention that the claim of America being
supplied with foreign molasses instead of from the British colonies
is false. The British plantations used almost all their molasses for the
production of high-quality rum that was destined for Great Britain.

The petition continues with what for the story of this prologue is
a side issue: "as well as [being supplied] with foreign European goods
and manufactures, contrary to the intention of the laws in being [the
Navigation Acts, or Acts of Trade and Navigation]." This mention
of illicit European trade is a prelude to an issue that will become important later in the story of the Sugar Act.

Here is the end of the petition:

As that *new method of trade encreased and enriched the colonies
of other nations,* so it was injurious to the trade of this kingdom,
and greatly impoverished the British Sugar-Colonies; and therefore
the Petitioners prayed the consideration of the House, and such
relief as the House should think fit.[3]

The House of Commons on March 26 considered the Sugar Bill
of 1731.

The title:

[An Act] for the better Securing and Encouraging the Trade of his Majesty's Sugar Colonies in America.[4]

The preamble. There is no doubt about the favored colonies:

Whereas the Welfare and Prosperity of his Majesty's Sugar Colonies in America, are of the greatest Consequence and Importance to the Navigation, Strength, and Wealth of this Kingdom: And whereas, of late Years a Trade has been carried on by divers of his Majesty's Subjects on the Continent of America to the Foreign Sugar Colonies there, to the great Prejudice and Discouragement of his Majesty's said Sugar Colonies. For remedy whereof. . . .[5]

The remainder of the preamble makes it clear the plan of the bill is to secure and encourage the trade of the British sugar colonies by preventing American trade with the foreign colonies.

The bill contained a two-part solution: prohibit imports, prohibit exports. First,

Section I. *No sugar, rum or melasses of the plantations of foreign nations shall be imported* into Britain or Ireland, or to any of the King's dominions in America.

Sugar and rum were important imports, but—to the Americans—the vital issue was the prohibition of molasses because of its importance to the economy of New England and New York.

Second,

Section VII. Whereas great numbers of horses and great quantities of lumber have been exported from our Continent colonies to the foreign sugar colonies, whereby they are enabled more easily to carry on their said sugar plantations, none such were to be transported hereafter to those foreign colonies.[6]

This prohibition of the export of horses and lumber, prominent in the remedy proposed by Dunbar in late 1730, was intended to impede economic development of the foreign sugar colonies. While such an effect was to the benefit of the British plantations, it was a detriment to the Americans.

The British sugar interests could not have been more pleased with the bill. On April 14, the House of Commons passed the bill, but it later failed in the House of Lords over concerns about interference with trade.

Leading up to the 1732 session of Parliament there was another blizzard of polemical papers regarding trade between the Americans and the foreign sugar colonies. British planters repeated arguments of the previous year, requesting "Prohibition of the Importation of all Foreign Sugar, Rum and Molasses into any of his Majesty's Dominions," and "Prohibition of the British Subjects supplying the Foreign Sugar Colonies" with provisions that "tend to support and enlarge them."[7] On February 10, 1732, the Board of Trade characterized the situation this way. "The papers . . . consist of many allegations, but of allegations only, and not of proofs, which has brought this matter hitherto no farther than to an issue upon the facts in dispute between the opposite parties."[8]

Debate on the Sugar Bill of 1732 began on February 23 in the House of Commons. The title of the bill was the same as the bill of 1731. The prohibition against importing sugar, rum, and molasses (the 1731 section I) was retained, but the explicit prohibition of export of horses and lumber (the earlier section VII) was dropped. It was unnecessary. Since the trade was conducted on a barter basis—such as lumber for molasses—there was no market for the American exports once the foreign products were prohibited. The Americans, then and later, claimed that either a prohibition or a high duty on foreign molasses would "put a total stop to our exportation of lumber, horses, flour, and fish to the French and Dutch sugar colonies."[9]

An important point of debate was the claim of British planters that halting the export of materials from North America would hinder their French competition because the French could not easily obtain provisions from any other source. Taking the contrary position, and arguing against the bill, friend of America Sir John Barnard claimed that the French could obtain "all such necessaries from their colonies at Canada." And if that was not feasible, "they could have plenty of all those necessaries from France itself." He also pointed out that if Americans did not take their molasses, the French "would make their molasses into rum, and send it to Europe" and find other uses adverse to British interests.[10] After substantial further debate, on March 15 the bill passed and was sent up to the House of Lords. The Lords killed the bill, again as being detrimental to trade.

Following the defeat of the Sugar Bill, Richard Partridge (agent for Rhode Island, New York, and New Jersey) wrote Governor Wanton of Rhode Island about a West Indian plan to circumvent the House of Lords. In a previous letter, "I gave thee some acct relating to the passing the Sugar Bill in the House of Commons," and its defeat in the Lords, "so that there is an end of it for this year." But, he continues, describing a change in strategy, "I am told that it is intended next Sessions of Parliamt to lay a duty on Foreign Rum and Molasses imported into our Northn Colonies."[11]

It turns out that this is an ominous step. The previous prohibition is to be replaced by high duties having the same effect. They will be embedded in what is claimed to be a revenue act, a money bill. The duties were to be a sham, used to create a trade regulation in the form of a revenue measure—the sugar planters expecting the House of Lords thereby to defer to the House of Commons.

PART ONE

Duties for Trade Regulation

"[All statutes before 1764] are calculated to regulate trade, and preserve or promote a mutually beneficial intercourse between the several constituent parts of the empire; and though many of them imposed duties on trade, yet those duties were always imposed with design to restrain the commerce of one part that was injurious to another, and thus to promote the general welfare. The raising a revenue thereby was never intended."

—John Dickinson, December 1767

One

The Sugar Act of 1733

"That a Duty of 6d. [six pence] per Gallon, Sterling Money, be laid on all foreign Molosses and Syrups imported into any of his Majesty's Colonies or Plantations in America."
—A proposed duty, February 21, 1733

"The commons of Great Britain, assembled in Parliament, have *given and granted unto your Majesty* the several and respective rates and duties hereinafter mentioned."
—The Sugar Act, May 17, 1733

THE SUGAR ACT OF 1733 LEVIED DUTIES ON FOREIGN SUGAR, rum, and molasses imported into the British colonies in North America. It was the first act of Parliament dealing with America that used words of donation typical of a revenue act: *giving and granting* revenue to the king. However, in a curious twist, the duties were not in fact intended to raise revenue, but to serve as regulation of trade—regulation supposedly to promote the general welfare but (as viewed by the Americans) to the benefit of British West Indian interests. The motivating factor behind the Sugar Act was the same as that of the sugar bills we saw in the prologue; it even had the identical title as those bills.[1] What had moved to the background, however, was the explicit intent to hinder development of the foreign plantations, to prevent them from producing sugar (in Dunbar's 1730 phrase) "in

the vast quantitys that at present glutt the European markets." Even
without that blunt objective—hidden by a pretense of preferential
tariffs—the purpose of the act remained ambiguous: Trade regulation? Revenue?

HOW THE ACT CAME ABOUT

The year 1733 was another busy one for attempts to influence Parliament by policy suggestions and polemical papers, reasons to pass
or prevent an act favorable to the British sugar colonies.[2]

In the House of Commons on February 21, 1733, friends of the
West Indian planters, instead of a prohibition as in prior years, proposed duties on foreign sugar, rum, and molasses.

> That a duty of 4s. [four shillings, later adjusted to five shillings]
> per hundred weight, Sterling Money, be laid on all foreign sugars
> and paneles [brown unpurified sugar], imported into any of his
> Majesty's colonies or plantations in America. This was agreed to
> without any opposition.
>
> That a Duty of 9d. per Gallon, Sterling Money, be laid on all
> foreign rum imported into any of his Majesty's colonies or plan-
> tations in America.
>
> That a Duty of 6d. [six pence] per Gallon, Sterling Money, be
> laid on all foreign Molosses and Syrups imported into any of his
> Majesty's Colonies or Plantations in America.

Sir John Barnard rose in opposition with a long speech, the gist
of which was to argue for small duties only, especially regarding the
duty on molasses.

> It ought to be only a small duty, for the sake of giving an advan-
> tage to our own sugar colonies in that respect, not such an high
> duty as was in a manner equal to a prohibition; for that was really
> granting a monopoly to our sugar-islands, with respect to a com-
> modity that is absolutely necessary for our northern colonies.

Advocates for the duties denied a prohibition, claiming the duties
were intended only to put the British sugar islands "on an equal foot
with the French."[3] The idea of a level playing field—or even a pref-

erential tariff ("giving an advantage to our own sugar colonies")—
was deceptive in regard to molasses; the Americans were already importing from the British islands as much molasses as was available.
The hidden intent of the act was to prohibit, by the levy of a high
duty, the import of foreign molasses (and export of supplies to the
foreign colonies). Putting matters on an equal foot had some validity
regarding the duty on sugar, balancing the duties on British sugar
levied by the Plantation Act of 1673. The rationale for such regulation of trade (in this bill using duties rather than prohibition) was
the same as that of 1731 and 1732; and as in those years, there was
an undertone of influence exerted by members of the House of Commons having significant financial interest in the success of plantations
in the West Indies. After further debate, the duties were agreed to.

On February 28, while the House of Commons was debating the
bill, Richard Partridge reported the result to Governor Wanton. He
characterizes the duties as taxation.

> This now comes to acquaint thee that thro the restlessness of the
> West India Gentlemen (who have the ministry on their side), the
> House of Commons have lately come into Resolutions to impose
> a duty upon Foreign Sugr, Molasses and Rum that shall be Im-
> ported into our Plantations [Rhode Island]. . . . I am of opinion if
> such a Law take place (besides the present Injury it will do), it will
> be rather worse in the consequence of it than the Bill of prohibi-
> tion last year, because of the levying a Subsidy upon a Free People
> without their Knowledge, agst their consent, who have the libertys
> and Immunitys granted them [of] Natural born Subjects.

He explains why it is worse—and is prescient about duties on imports being used as precedent for further taxation.

> *It may be drawn into a President for the future,* for by the same
> Rule that a British Parliamt imposes a duty on the Kings Subjects
> abroad, who have no Representatives in the State here, they may
> from 4*l* advance to 20*l*—to £100, on different things, and so ad
> infinitem which is an Infringemt on liberty and property and as I
> apprehend a violation of the Right of the Subject.[4]

In the House of Commons on March 8, Barnard moved to bring up a petition from Rhode Island against the bill. Thomas Winnington objected. "It has been a custom always observed in this House, not to receive any petitions against those Bills which were brought in for the laying on of any new duties." The resulting debate dealt not with the merits of the petition, but whether the petition should be heard. The central issue, bringing to the forefront the ambiguity of the bill, was whether the bill was a revenue measure or a trade regulation. Barnard made a sharp response to Winnington.

> Granting that it were a constant and perpetual rule not to receive petitions against such duties, yet certainly that rule could relate only to those duties which were to be laid on for raising money for the current service of the public, it could not be presumed to relate to those duties, which were to be laid on for the regulation of trade only; and this last is the case now before us.

He pointed out that it was inappropriate to treat the bill as a revenue measure; no one expects, or even wishes, "that any money shall be thereby raised for the use of the public."

> The Bill is not intended for any such end; it is rather *in the nature of a prohibition*, and it was never pretended that no petitions were ever to be received against a Bill for prohibiting any sort of commerce.

After further debate, "the question was put for bringing up the petition, which passed in the negative." This refusal to bring up the petition put the imprimatur of the House of Commons on the bill: a revenue measure. The bill passed and was sent up to the House of Lords on March 21.[5]

Partridge attempted to influence the Lords. On March 28, 1733, he wrote the Duke of Newcastle (then secretary of state) on behalf of his New York client.

> Inasmuch as there is a bill lately passt ye House of Commons [for imposing] high duties on ye importation of sugar etc. into ye Northern Colonys from ye Foreign Sugar Plantations and [the bill]

is likely to be brought up soon to ye House of Lords, the gentlemen of New York apprehend [in a petition] if it should pass into a law will be rather worse in the consequence of it than ye bill of prohibitions last year.

Besides ye injury, it will be off in itself almost tantamount to a prohibition. It is divesting them of their rights and privileges as ye King's natural born subjects and Englishmen in levying subsidies against their consent when they are annexed to no county in Great Britain, have no representatives in Parliament, nor any part of ye Legislature of this Kingdom, and that it will be drawn into a president hereafter whereby an incredible inconvenience may ensue.

He provides a reason the petition should be allowed.

And as we humbly conceive it will not be deem'd a breach of ye rules of ye house to hear us . . . as it is *not a common money bill* for raising a duty out of ye Kingdom, we pray this petition may be presented to ye House of Lords in a proper time after the bill has been read a first time.

I am, in behalf of the New York Gentlemen, Thy Friend, Richd. Partridge[6]

The letter highlights the intrinsic ambiguity of the bill. The duties are an inappropriate invasion of American rights as a tax ("levying subsidies against their consent"), but yet the Lords may consider the petition since the duties are not a tax, "not a common money bill."

When the Lords considered the bill, they took their responsibility seriously, investigating further and hearing petitions, but passed the bill on May 4. The act received the royal assent on May 17, 1733.

TEXT OF THE ACT

The Sugar Act of 1733 (6 George II c. 13)[7] laid duties on the importation of sugar, rum, and molasses from foreign sugar colonies.

The title:

An Act for the better Securing and Encouraging the Trade of his Majesty's Sugar Colonies in America.

This is the same title as the earlier bills, exposing the essential nature of the act: prohibition, not revenue.

The preamble:

Whereas, the welfare and prosperity of your Majesty's sugar colonies in America are of the greatest consequence and importance to the trade, navigation, and strength of this kingdom; and whereas . . .

The British sugar colonies have problems:

the planters of the said sugar colonies have of late years fallen under such great discouragements, that they are unable to improve or carry on the sugar trade upon an equal footing with the foreign sugar colonies, without some advantage and relief be given to them from Great Britain;

The solution:

for remedy whereof, and for the good and welfare of your Majesty's subjects, we, your Majesty's most dutiful and loyal subjects, the commons of Great Britain, assembled in Parliament, *have given and granted* unto your Majesty the several and respective rates and duties hereinafter mentioned, and in such manner and form as is hereinafter expressed.

Supporting the trickery of a revenue act, the preamble has words of donation typical of bills imposing taxation: given and granted.

Then the duties: "that it may be enacted, and be it enacted by the king's most excellent majesty . . . that from and after [December 25, 1733],"

Rum, ninepence per gallon.

there shall be raised, levied, collected and paid unto and for the use of his Majesty, his heirs and successors, upon all rum or spirits of the produce or manufacture of any of the [foreign colonies which shall be imported] the sum of nine pence, money of Great Britain . . . for every gallon thereof;

Molasses, sixpence per gallon. This was the most important duty, placing a charge on a product vital to the economy of the northern continental colonies.

> and upon all molasses or syrups of such foreign produce or manufacture [which shall be imported] . . . the sum of six pence of like money for every gallon thereof;

Sugar, five shillings per hundredweight.

> and upon all sugars and paneles of such foreign growth, produce or manufacture, as aforesaid, which shall be imported . . . a duty after the rate of five shillings of like money, for every hundred weight Avoirdupoize.

This rate sets the duty on foreign white sugar to be the same as the plantation duty on British white sugar. For British brown sugar (bearing a plantation duty of only one shilling and six pence), the rate acts as a preferential tariff.

Section 2.

> II. [Duties] shall be paid down in ready money by the importers thereof, before the landing of the [commodities].

Section 3. John Adams much later wrote that "the third section [makes this] the most arbitrary among statutes that were all arbitrary, the most unconstitutional among laws which were all unconstitutional."[8] It first deals with forfeiture.

> III. That in case any of the said commodities shall be landed or put on shore . . . before the duties by this act charged or chargeable thereupon shall be duly paid, or without [appropriate papers], all such goods or the value of the same, shall be forfeited;

Goods to be seized.

> And all and every such goods as shall be so landed or put on shore, contrary to the true intent and meaning of this act, shall, and may be seized by the governor or commander-in-chief . . . or by any custom-house officer, impost, or excise officer.

Courts of admiralty have jurisdiction.

And all and every such offense and forfeitures shall and *may be prosecuted for and recovered in any court of admiralty* in his majesty's colonies or plantations in America (which court of admiralty is hereby authorized, empowered, and required to proceed to hear, and finally determine the same), or in any court of record [common-law court] in the said colonies or plantations where such offence is committed, *at the election of the informer or prosecutor.*

Americans objected to admiralty courts because their use violated the right to trial by jury. (The judge rules not only on matters of law but also on matters of fact—the role of juries in common-law courts.) The British had good reason for the establishment of such courts: the difficulty in obtaining convictions from a jury in common-law courts.[9] It was widely believed in Great Britain that, as one British official in America put it in 1743, "a trial by jury here is only trying one illicit trader by his fellows, or at least his well-wishers."[10]

Products of the prosecution are apportioned in three parts.

Penalties and forfeitures so recovered there shall be divided as follows; viz. one third part thereof for the use of his Majesty, his heirs and successors, to be applied for the support of the government of the colony or plantation where the same shall be recovered, one third part to the governor or commander in chief of the said colony or plantation, and the other third part to the informer or prosecutor who shall sue for the same.

Section 4 deals with importation of specified goods into Ireland.

Section 5 sets penalties for assisting in unlawful importation, even for simply knowingly receiving into "their house or custody, any of the commodities aforementioned."

Section 6 specifies penalties "if any person or persons shall hinder, molest, or resist, any custom-house officer." It also specifies penalties "if any officer or officers of the customs or excise [shall] connive at the fraudulent importation [of any commodities] contrary to the purport and true meaning of this act."

In addition, and a grievance of American merchants, section 6 provides protection to a customs officer against suit by the owner of the ship or commodities seized.

> VI. And if any officer or officers of the customs, impost or excise officer or officers, or their assistants, shall be sued or prosecuted for any thing done in execution of his or their duty for the better and more effectual putting in force this present act, he or they may and *shall plead the general issue*, and give this act and the special matter in evidence, and the *judges shall allow thereof*;[11]

Section 7 is specific to those in charge of a ship or vessel. It sets the penalty for facilitating illegal importation—and in addition extends jurisdiction of the act beyond seaborne trade.

> VII. That if any of his Majesty's subjects, who is or shall be master, or have the charge of any ship or vessel, shall take in, or permit or suffer to be taken in, at sea or in any *creek or harbour, or other place*, any sugar, paneles, syrups or molasses, rum or spirits, in order to be . . . brought on shore and landed in any of his Majesty's plantations in America . . . shall forfeit and pay the sum of one hundred pounds.

Section 8 places the burden of proof on the owner of the commodities seized. That is, the accused must show papers attesting to the legal nature of the cargo.

> VIII. That upon all suits and prosecutions . . . for the bringing on shore and landing of any of the commodities aforementioned in any of his Majesty's colonies or plantations in America, contrary to the purport and true meaning of this act, the *Onus probandi* [burden of proof] . . .

Proof of innocence can be that the commodities were shipped legally from Great Britain:

> that the same and every part thereof were fairly and bone fide and without fraud, loaden and shipped in Great Britain, in ships navigated according to the several laws in being in that behalf,

or were from the British sugar islands in the West Indies:

that all and every the commodities aforesaid, which shall be imported into any of his Majesty's colonies or plantations in America, were of the growth, produce or manufacture of his Majesty's colonies or plantations there,

or all duties were paid:

were duly entered, and had really and bona fide paid the duties hereby charged and chargeable thereon, before the bringing on shore and landing thereof in any of his Majesty's colonies or plantations in America,

Here lies the burden of proof:

shall lie on the claimer or owner thereof.

Section 9 provides for repayment of British import duties when sugar is re-exported. Import duties on "sugar or paneles of the growth, produce or manufacture of any of the colonies or plantations belonging to or in the possession of his Majesty [shall] be repaid to such merchant or merchants, who do export the same."

Section 10 provides a partial refund of British import duties for sugars refined in Great Britain, on condition that "the said sugar so exported was produced from brown and muscovado sugar . . . imported from some of the [British] colonies or plantations in America."

Sections 11 and 12 deal with time limits for prosecution and provide for the expense of prosecution to be paid out of penalties and forfeitures adjudged.

Section 13 provides for special favorable treatment of some sugars from Spain and Portugal.

The act ends, containing in total fourteen sections, with a time limitation of five years, hence requiring periodic reenactment (which was routinely done by Parliament).[12]

This "Address of Assembly of Barbados to the King" in August 1733 illustrates the delight of the British sugar islands with the act.

"The passing that law is justly apprehended as a signall and most valuable instance of your Majesty's paternal care and concern for your Sugar Colonyes, who now entertain hopes through the blessing of God and your Majesty's favour and protection, of being restored to a flourishing condition."[13] My point in highlighting the relationship between the sugar colonies and the king is to emphasize the importance to Great Britain of the colonies in the West Indies. At this time, the West Indies sugar islands were the most valuable of Great Britain's possessions in America. Their value was not only in revenue produced but in that they were important to the economy of the continental colonies.[14]

NATURE OF THE ACT

Looking at how the act was developed and debated, it is clear that treating the bill as a revenue measure was simply a ruse to facilitate its passage. The true purpose was the same as the Sugar Bills of 1731 and 1732: trade regulation, specifically prohibition. The resulting ambiguity was long-lasting and worthy of learned commentary.

In 1774, Edmund Burke asserted in the House of Commons that the title was more important than the words of the preamble. "The title of this Act of George the 2nd, notwithstanding the words of donation [in the preamble], considers it merely as a *regulation of trade.*"[15]

Pamphleteer John Lind, writing on behalf of the government, expressed a contrary view. He criticized Burke's analysis, and asserted that the words of donation did make this an act of revenue. "The act uses the technical words of 'give, and grant.' Here then at least, one would think, was clearly a duty imposed for the purpose of raising a revenue."[16]

There is the ambiguity: "regulation of trade" vs. "raising a revenue." The ambiguity lays the foundation for later controversy. Despite most British officials coming to understand the act as a regulation of trade, in 1763 it became useful for British leaders (when preparing to enforce and renew the act) to view its purpose as being raising revenue.

LACK OF ENFORCEMENT

American merchants thought the sixpence molasses duty exorbitant, effectively a prohibition. But in the event, the duty never did much to restrict American commerce; through bribery and smuggling the Americans imported the molasses they needed—at a cost of about one penny per gallon. The smuggling was facilitated by the fact that the act was difficult to enforce; Governor Belcher of Massachusetts wrote the Board of Trade on March 2, 1737.

> The Sea Coast of the Province is so extensive & has so many Commodious harbours, that the small number of Custom House Officers are often complaining they are not able to do much for preventing illegal Trade.[17]

The British sugar planters were not happy with the lack of enforcement, but this was the era later called "wise and salutary neglect." From time to time, British officials admonished the Americans to adhere to the act and threatened to enforce it, but nothing ever came of such nagging.

ILLICIT TRADE DURING THE WAR

In the midst of the Seven Years' War, American commerce with the French West Indies was a serious offense; it was trading with the enemy in violation of laws passed to that effect. In early 1759, the Lords of Trade requested a report from the customs commissioners. Their report of May 10 addressed these points.

> 1. The illicit Importation of *Rum and Molasses* from the French Islands into the British Northern Colonies.
> 2. The importation of goods from different parts of Europe (particularly Holland and Hamburgh) into North America, and the carrying Enumerated goods from thence to the said places, and others in Europe, *contrary to Law, whereby all such Imports and Exports are restrained to Great Britain only.*

The report's elaboration of the first point reinforces the fact that, by this time, the Sugar Act was widely understood to be a regulation of trade.

> So long as the high Duty on Foreign Rum, Sugar, and Molasses (*then intended, We Apprehend, as a Prohibition*) continues, the

running of these Goods into His Majesty's Northern Colonies will be unavoidable, notwithstanding all the Orders that have been given or may be given to prevent it; and yet it is extremely difficult to foresee how far it may be expedient to attempt to remedy this Evil by an alteration of this Law which was passed at the request of the British Planters, as an Encouragement to their Trade.

Discussion of the second point starts out with the *importation* of goods into North America—the trade noted as early as 1730 in the essay by Mr. Dunbar (the illicit importation of "foreign European goods and manufactures"). "The great extent of the Coast very much favors the running through, before the Masters make their Reports at the Customshouses." Then, regarding *exportation*:

> With respect to Enumerated Goods exported from the Northern Colonies, in case the Ships that clear out, from thence for Great Britain, will be guilty of Frauds and deviation by carrying their Goods to other places in Europe than Great Britain, it is impossible for the Officers of the Customs in the Plantations to prevent it [and when legal action is taken, the] prosecutions must be carried on in the ordinary course of proceeding in the Colonies, *where it is apprehended, that Verdicts upon points of this Nature are not so impartial as in England.*[18]

On August 23, 1760, Secretary of State William Pitt directed the governors in North America to prevent smuggling. He characterized it as "an Illegal and most pernicious Trade" and governors were to "take every Step authorized by Law to bring all such heinous Offenders to the most exemplary and condign Punishment."[19] In addition, Pitt made effective use of Royal Navy vessels in stopping illicit trade. Demonstration that the Royal Navy could be effective in such a role influenced British actions a few years later. Pitt was famous then from his conduct of the Seven Years' War, and later a distinguished statesman and brilliant speaker in the House of Commons.

The pretense of a revenue act—duties being used in place of prohibition, the use of words of donation, and the deceptive vote of the House of Commons in 1733 to refuse consideration of a petition—made the act a fraud, the duties a sham, all in order to conceal that it was trade regulation. Over time the purpose of the act became obscure, creating ambiguity—trade regulation versus revenue—that cast a long shadow. That the British eventually chose to treat it as a revenue act, while the Americans continued to see it as trade regulation, contributed to the controversy beginning in 1764.

Two

Revise and Enforce

"The Military Establishment necessary for maintaining these Colonies requires a large Revenue to support it, [and] their vast Increase in Territory and Population makes the proper Regulation of their Trade of immediate Necessity."
—George Grenville, 1763

A T THE VICTORIOUS CONCLUSION OF THE SEVEN YEARS' WAR IN 1763, the British saw two problems. First, it was necessary to retain a substantial force of British regular army regiments in the colonies in order to provide for the defense and protection of the North American territory so dramatically expanded by French and Spanish concessions. In order to not further burden British taxpayers already paying heavy taxes to support the debt resulting from the war, it was necessary that America provide financial support for those troops, to bear their fair share of the burden. Second, it had become clear that the American colonies were drifting away from what was perceived as a necessary subservience to the mother country. The most obvious factor was American disregard for the laws of trade: clandestine trade with Europe in violation of the Navigation Acts, and smuggling goods from foreign islands in the West Indies in violation of the Sugar Act of 1733. It seemed as though the problems could be solved only by a drastic change in colonial policy.[1]

British leaders decided that the Sugar Act of 1733, revised and enforced, could be used to draw the necessary revenue from America,
and would be an ideal vehicle for the establishment of regulations
that would facilitate strict enforcement of the laws of trade. Those
decisions—draw revenue from America and reinvigorate the laws of
trade—inaugurated a change in colonial policy. Americans took a
dim view of the change. In October 1774, the First Continental Congress wrote, "Soon after the conclusion of the late war, there commenced a memorable change in the treatment of these Colonies. . . .
By a statute made in the fourth year of the present reign . . . the Commons of Great-Britain undertook to give and grant to his Majesty
many rates and duties to be paid in these Colonies. To enforce the
observance of this Act, it prescribes a great number of severe penalties and forfeitures." John Adams wrote in his diary in March 1774
that "the conspiracy was first regularly formed and begun to be ex-
ecuted in 1763 or 4."[2]

THE GRENVILLE PROGRAM

In April of 1763, George Grenville became First Lord of the Treasury
and prime minister. Although it fell to Grenville's administration to
deal with decisions made over the previous year, the changes he put
into place stamped his own imprint on events to follow, now widely
known as the Grenville program.[3]

On May 21, Charles Jenkinson (a principal secretary in the Treasury) wrote the office of the customs commissioners that "the revenues arising from the duties of customs in America and the West
Indies amount in *no degree to the sum which might be expected* from
them." He directed them "to find out the causes of this deficiency"
and to report "in what manner the revenue [might] be better collected
in the future."[4]

It was at this point that British leaders began treating the act of
1733 as if it were, in fact, intended to raise revenue. There was little
basis for such treatment. Although the House of Commons had
adopted in 1733 the pretense of a revenue bill, we saw the apt re-
joinder from Sir John Barnard pointing out that it was inappropriate
to treat the bill as a revenue measure in that *no one expects, or even
wishes,* "that any money shall be thereby raised for the use of the

public." The history and title of the act expose that the intent had been to impose trade restrictions. Further, we have seen that British officials understood the purpose of the duties to be, "then intended, We Apprehend, as a Prohibition."

On June 1, the Privy Council directed implementation of the Hovering Act (3 George III c. 22), a recently passed statute earlier sponsored by Grenville as First Lord of the Admiralty. The long title of the act is: "An act for the further improvement of his Majesty's revenue of customs; and for the encouragement of officers making seizures; and for the prevention of the clandestine running of goods into any part of his Majesty's dominions." The act provided for British warships to be used in enforcement, empowering officers of the Royal Navy to act as customs officers; it encouraged the commanders to be diligent, even aggressive. "For the more effectual prevention of the infamous practice of smuggling, it may be necessary to employ several of the ships and vessels of war belonging to his Majesty." The proceeds of any seizure were to be divided "amongst all such officers and seamen of such ship or vessel of war who shall make any such seizure."[5] On June 21, the Lords of the Admiralty ordered additional vessels to join the fleet in American waters, and ordered commanders of ships in the American fleet to strictly enforce the laws of trade. These actions resulted in improved enforcement of the Sugar Act of 1733 even before revisions to the act established improved regulatory mechanisms.

The Jenkinson letter of May 21 and follow-up inquiries brought forth a flow of information. The final report from the customs commissioners on September 16—a report that much influenced the resulting Sugar Act—pointed out that trade with the West Indies sugar plantations was destined to grow; the continental colonies, "being now augmented, will require very great additional quantities of sugar, rum, and molasses for their own necessary consumption." The likely source for the products would be the French islands, "where these commodities will be likely to be obtained at the cheapest rate." The commissioners recommended that revenue could be increased by charging "proper duties thereon at a lower rate than at present, so as to diminish the temptation to smuggling." (As recently as March

30, Grenville, while still First Lord of the Admiralty, had debated in the House of Commons in favor of keeping the duty at a rate of sixpence, but this report was influential in changing his thinking.) The commissioners also reported illicit trade with Europe. British ships "frequently arrive" in America from foreign European ports after presenting false claims (during the required stop at a British port) about destination of goods, claiming that their cargo was primarily destined for "some foreign settlement." A typical ploy was to enter "only a few boxes or bales of goods" for ports in the British colonies and thereby obtain "legal clearances for these colonies and admission thereby to our American ports." Once having such access, the ships would illicitly unload their entire cargo.[6] The illicit trade with the manufacturing countries of northern Europe was particularly detrimental, the Americans thereby receiving goods that should have been products of British manufacture.

By late September, Grenville had decided to revise the Sugar Act: reduce the molasses duty, add additional dutied products, appropriate the revenue to British forces in America, and establish regulations facilitating enforcement of the laws of trade. He sent a lengthy report to the Privy Council on October 4. This report is important, even famous, as it provided the basis for many provisions of the Sugar Act of 1764.

> We the Commissioners of your Majestys Treasury beg leave humbly to represent to your Majesty, that having taken into Consideration the present state of the Duties of Customs imposed on your Majestys Subjects in America and the West Indies, *we find, that the Revenue arising therefrom is very small and inconsiderable having in no degree increased with the Commerce of those Countries*, and is not yet sufficient to defray a fourth Part of the Expence necessary for collecting it. We observe with concern that through Neglect, Connivance and Fraud, not only the Revenue is impaired, but the Commerce of the Colonies is diverted from its natural Course and the salutary Provisions of many wise Laws [the Navigation Acts] to *secure it to the Mother Country* are in great Measure defeated.

The idea behind "secure it to the Mother Country" is important. British leaders were not simply concerned that illicit trade was reducing revenue but that it threatened the connection between Great Britain and the colonies.

After further discussion about the need for revenue and the British forces to be retained in America, the analysis reaches this conclusion.

> Their vast Increase in Territory and Population makes the proper Regulation of their Trade of immediate Necessity, lest the continuance and extent of the dangerous Evils abovementioned may render all Attempts to remedy them hereafter infinitely more difficult, if not utterly impracticable. We have endeavoured therefore to discover, and as far as the Power of our Department will allow, remove the Causes, to which the *Deficiency of this Revenue and the contraband Trade with other European Nations are owing.*[7]

The belief of British leaders in widespread illegal trade with Europe motivated many of the regulations later prescribed by the Sugar Act. The resulting restrictions had an adverse impact on American commerce and led to substantial conflict between American merchants and customs officers. As a consequence, the regulations—compounded by the use of the Royal Navy for enforcement—contributed a great deal to the animosity between Great Britain and America, and ultimately to the Revolution. It is not clear whether or not there was, in fact, widespread contraband trade with Europe—but British leaders believed that to be the case.[8]

The report also described action Grenville had already taken and made recommendations for action by Parliament. On October 5, the Privy Council issued an Order in Council as complete acceptance of—and direction to implement—the report of the previous day. Grenville initiated action to prepare a draft bill for the revised Sugar Act.

An important early step was to determine the rate for the molasses duty. The West Indies sugar planters pushed for a duty of four pence per gallon, while the Americans wanted a penny, or at the limit no more than two pence per gallon. Grenville turned to numbers; he started with an estimate that, at a duty of twopence, the annual legal importation of foreign molasses would be eight million gallons per year. He then calculated the income likely to be produced by various rates (allowing that the higher the duty the less molasses would be legally imported), finally settling on three pence as the rate that would maximize revenue. Another important decision made by Grenville was how the funds were to be appropriated. For a few months he considered applying the funds to the support of the civil administration (for example, the salaries of governors) as well as the military but eventually settled on support of military costs only.[9]

On January 9, 1764, Jenkinson requested from William Wood, secretary to the Board of Customs, an accounting of various duties that had been collected. Wood provided the information the next day and also offered an unsolicited cautionary thought. All the plans "respecting the Plantations [should] be deferred to another year," except a simple continuation of the act of 1733. It would be wise to defer new duties since the ministry was lacking an "account [of] what Duties are payable by any Act of Assembly, in any of the British Plantations, in America, on the importation, and exportation of . . . any goods, or merchandize."[10] This was a rare hesitation about immediate implementation of American taxation. William Wood's observation about lack of information about duties established by the colonial assemblies was directly on point but his advice ignored: preparation of the bill continued apace. At this point a draft bill had been prepared, largely the work of John Tyton, solicitor to the customs, and Robert Yeates, a clerk in the treasury office; the final bill was not completed until involvement of the committee of ways and means in March.

NEWS TO AMERICA

In parallel with development of the Grenville program, Americans received updates regarding events in London. On May 30, 1763, the *New York Gazette* and the *Newport Mercury* reported a letter from London dated March 27. It deals with the method of raising money to support the British regiments in America.

> The money, it is said, will be levied by Act of Parliament, and *raised on a Stamp duty*, excise on rum distilled on the continent,

and a duty on foreign sugar and molasses etc. by reducing the former duty on these last-mentioned articles, which it is found impracticable to collect, to such a one as will be collected.

The writer was not much concerned with duties on foreign sugar and molasses but does express dread of taxes other than customs duties.

This manner of raising money, except what may arise on the foreign sugars, &c., I apprehend, will be thought greatly to diminish even the appearance of the subject's liberty, since nothing seems to be more repugnant to the general principles of freedom than the subjecting a people to taxation by laws in the enactment of which they are not represented.[11]

On August 3, Massachusetts Governor Francis Bernard wrote the politically well-connected Richard Jackson in London with concern about renewal and enforcement. (Jackson was London agent for Connecticut and Pennsylvania, legal counsel to the Massachusetts agents, and later a Massachusetts agent himself.) Bernard uses the name *Melasses Act*. (By 1763, similar designations were often used for the Sugar Act of 1733.)

The Danger of the Melasses Act being renewed & carried into full execution is Very alarming. The mischeivous consequences of such a Measure, I fear, will not appear so certain on your side of the Water as they do here. . . . If the Northern Colonies are not allowed to import foreign Sugars & Melasses upon Practicable terms, they will become desperate.[12]

Massachusetts Lieutenant Governor Thomas Hutchinson also wrote Jackson on August 3.

The Molosses Act as it now stands was undoubtedly intended to have the force of a prohibition. To reduce the duty to a *penny per gallon* I find would be generally agreeable to the people here & the Merchant would readily pay it, but do they see the consequence. Will not this be introductory to taxes duties & excises upon other articles & would this consist with the so much esteemed privilege of English Subjects the being taxed by their own representatives?[13]

In a letter to the Board of Trade on September 5, Bernard gave his reasons against enforcement.

The best of Cod goes to Spain Portugal & Italy, the produce whereof is chiefly remitted to England; the Worst sort is sent to the West Indies. . . . These several kinds of fish together with boards staves shingles & hoops commonly called lumber, with some provisions . . . make up the freights to the West Indies: the returns are made partly in remittances to England & partly in rum, Sugar & Melasses. The latter Article . . . is distilled into rum, which is used in the trade . . . & some part (perhaps too much) consumed by the inland inhabitants. But upon the Whole, *I consider the Melasses distilling as very necessary to the chief part of the trade of this province*; and if it should be obstructed either by a severe execution of the present laws or by the enacting of new ones for that purpose, I fear that the *consequences would soon be felt by the English Merchants trading to this Country*.[14]

The first official notice of Grenville's intent to strictly enforce the laws of trade was a circular letter to colonial governors from Secretary of State Egremont. It arrived in Boston on September 14.

July 9, 1763
It having appeared, that the Publick Revenue has been greatly diminished, and the fair Trader much prejudiced, by the fraudulent Methods used to introduce into His Majesty's Dominions . . . Commodities of Foreign Growth, in National, as well as Foreign, Bottoms, by means of small Vessels hovering on the Coasts; And that this iniquitous Practice has been carried to a great Heighth in America; an Act was passed the last Session of Parliament [the Hovering Act] by which the former Laws, relative to this Matter, are enforced, and extended to the British Dominions in all Parts of the World.

Eventually, Egremont gets to the action required: the governors are directed "to put an effectual Stop to the clandestine Running of Goods into any place within your Jurisdiction."

> The King wishes that all possible Means should be used to root out so iniquitous a Practice; a Practice carried on in Contravention of many express & repeated Laws, [leading] to the *Diminution & Impoverishment of the Public Revenue.*

Egremont goes on and on, explaining other enforcement actions taken by the ministry. At the end, he further emphasizes the importance to the king of "Improvement of the Public Revenue." It is a matter on which "His Majesty lays so much stress."[15] That Egremont repeatedly emphasizes improving the revenue is a hint that something new is going on, implying that the direction from the king is not simply another empty exhortation to adhere to the laws of trade. (For example, trade instructions of January 1758 from King George II to the newly appointed governor of New Jersey included this specific admonition to enforce the Sugar Act of 1733. "And whereas by [the Sugar Act] a Duty is laid on all Rum, Melasses, Syrups, Sugar and Paneles of [foreign colonies], notwithstanding which we are informed that great Quantities of foreign Rum, Melasses, Syrups, Sugars and Paneles are Clandestinely landed in Our plantations without payment of the said Duty, Our Will & Pleasure is, that you be aiding and assisting to the Collectors [i.e., Collectors of his Majesty's customs] . . . "[16] Such instruction to newly appointed governors was routine.)

On October 28, Thomas Cushing (a patriot leader and influential member of the Massachusetts House of Representatives), wrote Massachusetts agent Jasper Mauduit, starting with more concern about the Hovering Act.

> I now take the Liberty to write you upon a subject that very nearly affects the trade of this Province. It's relative to an Act of Parliament passed the last session Intituled *an Act for the further improvement of his majesty's Revenue of Customs* . . . in pursuance of which Act a Number of men of warr have been Stationed upon these Coasts, the Captains of which . . . *have strict orders rigor-*

ously to execute the Act of Parliament pass'd in the year 1733, laying a Duty upon all foreign Mollasses, Rum and Sugar; this has much Alarm'd us as it is Sudden and unexpected.

He emphasizes the disruption that is sure to follow enforcement.

The Rigourous execution of this Act laying a duty on molasses, etc., will be extremely prejudicial if not altogether *destructive to the trade of this and the neighboring Governments.* It demands therefore our greatest Attention and I doubt not the General Court at the next session will fully Instruct you upon this Head. In the mean time, it is presumed, that you (together with the other Agents of the Northern Colonies) will exert yourself upon this occasion, and when the Parliament meet endeavour to gett this Act repealed or, in some way or other, obtain reliefs for us under this insupportable Burden.[17]

By late 1763 it was clear to Americans that Grenville was going to call for a tax to support British troops in America, and that such a tax was going to be levied by Parliament. A complex part of the consequent controversy over taxation was the distinction between duties collected at American ports (often called *external taxes*), long recognized by the colonists as being within the rightful authority of Parliament, and *internal taxes* such as excise taxes or a stamp duty. This issue was brought up by Richard Jackson. On December 27, he wrote to Benjamin Franklin (who was then a member of the Pennsylvania committee of correspondence).

A Revenue to be raised in America for the Support of British Troops is not now to [be] argued against: it would answer no Purpose to do so. . . . It is not disputed that [each mother country] is Mistress of the Trade of its Colonys: this Right has always been . . . exercised by England and all other Countries; [since the mother country] may prohibit foreign Trade, *it may therefore tax it.* And the Colonys have a Compensation in Protection, *but I dread internal Taxes.*[18]

Now is the time for a word of caution about the vocabulary of contemporary speeches and letters. There are a number of words and phrases important to the Sugar Act discussion that are used in vague and confusing ways: taxes, external taxes, port duties (i.e., duties collected at an American port), customs, customs duties (paid to the "collector of his Majesty's customs"), duties, and regulation of trade (using duties). Such phrases were (at least for a few years) often used in contrast to internal taxes, those taxes affecting the internal polity of a colony. The American distinction between internal and external taxation—and what British leaders thought was the American distinction—played a role in the story of the Sugar Act.

Eventually the high-level commands reached officials charged with putting them into execution.

> Custom-House, Port of Salem, New Jersey, Dec. 26, 1763.
> Whereas it has been represented to the Lords Commissioners of His Majesty's Treasury, that many Vessels, trading to Plantations not belonging to the King of Great Britain, and returning with Cargoes of Rum, Sugar and Molasses, have found Means to smuggle the same into His Majesty's Plantations, without paying the King's Duty: This is to inform all Masters of Vessels using the said Trade, that they are hereby strictly required, on their Arrival here, to enter or report their Ships and Cargoes at the Custom-House, when proper Officers will be put on board such Vessels, to see that the Act of the Sixth of His late Majesty, King George the Second (imposing a Duty on all foreign Rum, Sugar and Molasses) be in all its Parts fully carried into Execution.
> By Order of the Surveyor-General,
> Francis Hopkinson, Collector[19]

Collectors at other ports in the northern colonies made similar announcements. (The position of collector of his Majesty's customs is of considerable importance, playing a major role in enforcement of the Sugar Act.)

By this time, enforcement actions were having a detrimental effect on American commerce. Bernard wrote Richard Jackson on January 7, 1764.

The publication of orders for the strict execution of the Melasses Act has caused a [great] alarm in this Country . . . Petitions from the trading Towns have been presented to the general Court, and a large committee of both houses is setting every day to prepare instructions for their Agent. In the Mean time the Merchants say, there is an end of the trade of this Province; that it is sacrificed to the West Indian Planters.[20]

On June 1, Benjamin Franklin wrote Richard Jackson that "The Men of War station'd in our several Ports are very active in their new Employment of Custom house Officers; a Portmanteau cannot go between here [Philadelphia] and New York without being search'd. Every Boat stopt and examin'd, and much Incumbrance by that means brought upon all Business.[21]

Although the Americans were coming to understand that the Sugar Act of 1733 was, in fact, this time going to be enforced, there was still no reason to realize that the enforcement was simply the opening scene of a soon-to-be-enacted constitutional drama.

Three

Reasons Against the Renewal

"As the Act, commonly called the Sugar Act, has been passed upwards of thirty years without any Benefit to the Crown . . . the following Considerations are offered as Reasons why it should not be renewed."

—Boston merchants, 1763

BASED ON REPORTS EARLY IN 1763 FROM MASSACHUSETTS AGENT Jasper Mauduit, Boston merchants were apprehensive about British plans for the Sugar Act. On April 14, the merchants formally organized the *Society for Encouraging Trade and Commerce within the Province of Massachusetts Bay*. The stated purpose of the society was to prevent the renewal of the Sugar Act. Implicit in objection to renewal was protest against enforcement, which by late 1763 was having an adverse effect on commerce, even seen as threatening destruction of American trade. The merchants took no formal action to prevent renewal or protest enforcement until late in the year, but their writings and letters to like-minded merchants in other colonies then prompted further protest.

THE PROTESTS

In December, the Boston merchants drew up a memorial stating reasons against renewal and enforcement of the Sugar Act of 1733. It was presented to the Massachusetts General Court on December 27,

"praying that his Excellency and Honors would take into Consideration the Act of Parliament known by the Name of the Sugar Act . . .
and make such Application for their Relief as they in their great Wis-
dom shall judge best."[1]

> As the Act, commonly called the Sugar Act, has been passed up-
> wards of thirty years without any Benefit to the Crown, the Duties
> arising from it, having never been appropriated by Parliament to
> any particular Use; and as this Act will expire this Winter, the fol-
> lowing Considerations are offered as Reasons why it should not
> be renewed.

Enforcement of the act will put an end to all trade with the foreign
islands.

> FIRST, It is apprehended that the Trade is so far from being able
> to bear the high Duties imposed by this Act, *that it will not bear
> any Duty at all.*[2]

Although the idea "that it will not bear any Duty at all" was
echoed by other colonies, as a practical matter it was understood that
the trade could withstand low duties, and particularly that a low molasses duty would not interfere with trade to the foreign islands. The
merchants explain that their export trade depends upon the barter
of provisions for sugar and molasses; it is a vital aspect of the commerce.

> The Price of Molosses at present, is but 12d Sterling per Gallon,
> at which Price it will barely answer to distil it into Rum for Ex-
> portation. Should this Duty be added, it would have the Effect of
> an absolute Prohibition on the Importation of Molasses and Sugar
> from the foreign Islands; and consequently the same effect on the
> Exportation of Fish, Lumber and other Commodities from hence
> to those Islands; as the French, Dutch and other Foreigners whom
> we supply with those Articles, *will not permit us to bring away
> their Money; so that unless we can take their ordinary Sugars and
> Molasses in Return, this Trade will be lost.*

Fishing is a vital industry. It stands on two legs: high quality fish to Europe and less desirable fish to the West Indies. Neither side of the business can stand alone.

SECONDLY, The Loss of the Trade to the foreign Islands, on which great Part of our other Trade depends, must greatly affect all the Northern Colonies, and entirely destroy the Fishery in this Province.

Since the British sugar islands take only a small portion of the undesirable fish, "the Remainder will be lost if we are prevented from supplying the foreign Islands, there being no other Market where it can be disposed of."

THIRDLY, A Prohibition on the Trade to foreign Islands will greatly promote the French Fishery: If the French Islands can be supplied with Fish for Molasses, it will be cheaper for them to purchase it of us than to catch it themselves.

But if American merchants cannot profitably trade fish for molasses, the French will expand their own fishery. And "their establishing such a Fishery will be very prejudicial to Great Britain."

FOURTHLY, The Fishery being a great Nursery of Seamen for his Majesty's Navy, the Destruction thereof must very much weaken the Naval Power of Great Britain.

And there are other adverse consequences. Trade of Great Britain:

FIFTHLY, The Destruction of the Fishery will be very prejudicial to the Trade of Great Britain by lessening the Demand for her Manufactures.

Trade of the colonies:

SIXTHLY, The Destruction of the Fishery will not only lessen the Importation of Goods from Great Britain, but must greatly prejudice the whole Trade of the Province. The Trade to the foreign Islands is become very considerable, [they being] supplied with Provisions, Fish, Lumber, Horses, Onions and other Articles ex-

ported from the Northern Colonies; for which we receive Molasses in Return; this is distilled into Rum for the Fishery, and to
export to the Southern Colonies.

Further, rum is vital for the trade with Africa, "to purchase Slaves
for our own Islands in the West-Indies."[3]

It is said by the [British] Planters in the West-Indies that they can
supply us with Rum and Molasses for the Fishery, and our own
Consumption . . . To which it may be answered [no they cannot].

Economy of the colonies:

SEVENTHLY, The Destruction of the Fishery will be the Ruin of
those concerned in that Business, and that are dependent on it.

The King's revenue:

EIGHTHLY, The Sugar Act, if put in Execution, will greatly affect
the King's Revenue, by lessening the Importation of Rum and
Sugar into Great Britain.

The Sugar Act works to benefit only a privileged few.

NINTHLY, This Act was procured by the Interest of the West-
India Planters, with no other View than to enrich themselves by
obliging the northern Colonies to take their whole Supply from
them.

The memorial ends with a summary of the situation, and a view
of the future.

Upon the whole, It is plain that our Islands are able neither to supply us with what we want from them, nor to take from us what
Lumber and Fish we are obliged to export: and they will be still
less able to do either; for our Demands will be growing faster than
their Produce, and our Fishery which has been increasing, will
continue still to increase, if not obstructed, while their Demands
have not increased in any Proportion, and never can.

On January 4, 1764, the Boston merchants wrote their counterparts in Rhode Island (and five days later, Connecticut) referring to the memorial as the *State of the Trade*.

The Act commonly known by the Name of the Sugar Act has long & justly been complain'd of by the Northern Colonies as a great Grievance; and should it be continued & put in Execution, with any Degree of Rigour (as is like to be the Case hereafter) it will give a mortal Wound to the Peace of these Colonies.

The merchants call for united action. "As this Act is now about to expire, it behoves us all to unite our endeavors to prevent, if possible, the revival of it."

To this Purpose the Merchants in this Town, sometime since, met together and chose a Committee to prepare a *State of the Trade* of this Province so far as it is affected by this act.

They explain that the Massachusetts General Court "will send the necessary Instructions to their Agent, and will oppose the Renewal of the Act to the utmost of their Power." They enclose the "State of the Trade," and look for assistance "in our Endeavours to defeat the iniquitous Schemes of these overgrown West Indians." (The influence of the West Indian lobby had waned over the last three decades, but many Americans incorrectly believed that the West Indians still had outsize ability to shape legislation.) In addition to actions of the General Court, "the Merchants here will severally write to their respective Correspondents in England & endeavour to convince them that the Act in Question is and will be prejudicial to the Trade of Great Britain."[4]

In the weeks following presentation to the General Court, the memorial was refined (principally in minor rephrasing), then printed as a pamphlet: *Reasons Against the Renewal of the Sugar Act.*[5] On February 10, the merchants sent 250 copies of the pamphlet to their counterparts in London, and also sent copies to other towns in Massachusetts and to neighboring colonies.

In mid-January, Rhode Island Governor Stephen Hopkins published an essay (*Providence Gazette*, January 14 and 21) laying out the harmful effect of the Sugar Act: *An Essay on the Trade of the Northern Colonies of Great Britain in North America.*

> The commerce of the British northern colonies in America is so peculiarly circumstanced, and from permanent causes, so perplexed and embarrassed, that it is a business of great difficulty to investigate it, and put it in any tolerable point of light.
>
> That which most particularly and unhappily distinguishes most of these northern British colonies from all others, either British or any other nation, is that the soil and climate of them is incapable of producing almost anything which will serve to send directly home to the mother country.

In addition, "their situation and circumstances are such as to be obliged to take off, and consume [great] quantities of British Manufactures." Having almost nothing to directly trade, purchases from Great Britain must be made with specie. The consequence is, "Unable to make remittances in a direct way, they are obliged to do it by a *circuity of commerce* unpracticed by and unnecessary in any other colony." When they cannot sell products for specie, they must be satisfied to "procure such things in return as may [require] several commercial exchanges to make a remittance home."

Exports start with fish from the northernmost colonies.

> [The fish] that are called merchantable are sent directly to Spain, Portugal, and Italy, and there sold for money or bills of exchange, which are sent directly to England. . . . A considerable part of the fish yet remaining, which is unfit for the European markets, serves for feeding the slaves in the West Indies; as much of this is sold in the English islands as they will purchase, and the residue sold in the French and Dutch Colonies, and in the end is turned into a remittance home.

"The colonies next to the southward" must rely on the circuity of commerce to transform exports into molasses, molasses into rum, and eventually into specie.

> Lumber, horses, pork, beef . . . [are] sold to the French and Dutch

for molasses; *this molasses is brought into these colonies, and there distilled into rum*, which is sent to the coast of Africa, and there sold for gold, ivory, and slaves: the two first of these are sent directly home; the slaves are carried to the English West-Indies and sold for money or bills of exchange, which are also remitted to England.

The essay was much-praised, reprinted by newspapers in Boston, New York, and Philadelphia, and later published (in London) as a pamphlet.[6]

In parallel with the Hopkins essay, Rhode Island merchants prepared a remonstrance against the renewal. It was completed on January 26 and—approved by the General Assembly—became the first American legislative protest against renewal of the Sugar Act: "To the Right Honorable the Lords Commissioners for Trade and Plantations."

The remonstrance points out that the result of trade with the foreign islands was the "import into this colony about fourteen thousand hogsheads of molasses." But much less from the British islands, "a quantity not exceeding twenty-five hundred hogsheads." Molasses was central to the economy of the colony; it "serves as an engine in the hands of the merchant to effect the great purpose of paying for British manufactures." Part of the molasses is traded to other colonies; "the remainder (besides what is consumed by the inhabitants) is distilled into rum, and exported to the coast of Africa."

Imports of British goods annually "amount at least to £120,000 sterling," while exports of "articles produced in the colony suitable for a remittance to Europe [amount only] to about £5,000 sterling, per annum."

The present price of molasses is about twelve pence, sterling, per gallon; at which rate, only, it can be distilled into rum for exportation; wherefore, if a duty should be laid on this article, the enhanced price may amount to a prohibition; and it may with truth be said, *that there is not so large a sum of silver and gold circulating in the colony*, as the duty imposed by the aforesaid act upon foreign molasses, would amount to in one year, which makes it absolutely impossible for the importers to pay it.

The remonstrance ends with, "it is submitted to Your Lordships, whether the renewal of the said law may not, instead of answering any useful purposes, be highly injurious to the interest both of Great Britain and these northern colonies."[7]

On January 20, Connecticut merchants presented a memorial to the General Assembly that "his Majesty has been pleased of late to Inforce the Execution of the Sugar Act," and that it "Expires about this time & will probably be again revived unless prevented by a Seasonable remonstrance on the part of the Northern Colonies." The merchants requested that Connecticut join with other colonies in remonstrating against enforcement and renewal of the act. The General Assembly took no timely action, but the merchants published a pamphlet later in the month: *Remarks on the Trade of the Colony*. The pamphlet was largely a repeat of material we have already seen.[8]

In February, New York merchants prepared a memorial in opposition to the renewal, and wrote merchants in Philadelphia, explaining their actions and that they were "heartily joining the eastern governments in soliciting a discontinuance of the most unjust of all laws, the Sugar Act."[9] The New York General Assembly acted on April 20, approving the memorial and sending it to the House of Commons. Reasons against renewal were advanced at great length, repeating the arguments of the other colonies. The economy of the northern colonies is dependent upon a *course of trade*, what Hopkins had called the circuity of commerce.

> Sugar and Molasses have been shewn to be the very Sinews of our Commerce, and the Sources from which, in a *Course of Trade*, we draw the most valuable Remittances; it would therefore seem necessary that they should be imported in Quantities Sufficient to supply the various Demands of our several commercial Interchanges, as well as our own Consumption; *but our Sugar Colonies are unable to afford this ample Supply*, nor if they were, could they take of our Produce, which alone would capacitate us to purchase it.

The General Assembly directed the colony's agent to "give all possible Opposition to the Renewal, or Continuation, of the said Act of the sixth of his late Majesty King George the Second."[10]

NATURE OF THE PROTESTS

The reasons advanced by the four northern colonies were the "first intercolonial movement of the pre-Revolutionary period designed to exert political pressure in England."[11] But they failed to prevent renewal: none of the protests of early 1764 arrived in London until it was too late to influence the debates on the Sugar Act. This did not mean that Grenville was unaware of the American opposition to the renewal; the London agents of the colonies were in contact with British officials.

The best representation of the American position was developed by Israel Mauduit (the brother and informal, unpaid assistant of Massachusetts agent Jasper Mauduit). Based on discussion throughout 1763, and especially on letters with guidance from Thomas Cushing, Israel prepared a document to be submitted to the Treasury, also signed by other colonial agents: *A Memorial to the Lords Commissioners of His Majesty's Treasury*. The memorial did not attempt to prevent the renewal; it instead put forth arguments that, in order to allow unhampered trade, no more than one penny per gallon should be levied. (But the memorial allowed that, deferring to the judgment of the Treasury, two pennies would be acceptable.)[12] The memorial was presented to and rejected by the Treasury on February 27. That was the last gasp of protests from the agents. Israel wrote a month later to explain that the agents felt further protest would antagonize and discourage friends of America in the House of Commons.

None of the protests made an appeal to constitutional issues. There was no complaint that American rights were violated, no claim that Parliament lacked authority to levy such duties. They addressed only the burden of the duties, consistently treating the Sugar Act of 1733 as a regulation of trade.[13] Here is the British view (in 1765) that the Americans made no constitutional objection to the Sugar Act of 1733.

> The Colonies have . . . acquiesced under several parliamentary Taxes. The 6 Geo. II. c. 13. . . . lays heavy Duties on all foreign Rum, Sugar, and Melasses imported into the British Plantations. The Amount of the Impositions has been complained of; the Policy of the Laws has been objected to; *but the Right of making such a Law, has never been questioned.*[14]

Not all British spokesmen agreed with Whately about American lack of objection to the right. "Page after page in the Journals [of the House of Commons] is filled with their objections to the principle of the act."[15]

Popular leader James Otis explained the American attitude in a pamphlet published in July 1764.

> The act of the 6th of his late Majesty, though it imposes a *duty* in terms, has been said to be designed for a *prohibition*, which is probable from the sums imposed; and 'tis pity it had not been so expressed, as there is *not the least doubt of the just and equitable right of the Parliament to lay prohibitions* through the dominions when they think the good of the whole requires it.[16]

British philosopher and pamphleteer Richard Price (more than a decade after Otis) was specific about the American response.

> In this act, the duties imposed are said to be given and granted by the Parliament to the King; and this is the first American act in which these words have been used. But notwithstanding this, as the act had the *appearance of being only a regulation of trade*, the colonies submitted to it.[17]

The fact that these reasons against renewal did not make a constitutional argument against the right of Parliament to levy duties for revenue opened the door to later British assertions that such duties—taxes, claimed the British—were acceptable to the Americans: that they objected to the policy but not the right of Parliament to make such a law. The colonies had a different viewpoint: they protested what they saw as exorbitant duties legitimately (if unwisely) imposed by Parliament to regulate trade.

There was some American recognition that the act might be used as a precedent for later taxation. Thomas Cushing wrote Jasper Mauduit late in January 1764. The General Court is of opinion that the act of 1733 "is at this time put in rigorous execution in order to obtain our Consent to some Dutys being laid, but this is look'd upon of dangerous consequence as it will be conceeding to the Parliaments having a Right to Tax our trade which we can't by any means think of admitting, as it would be contrary to a fundamentall Principall of our Constitution vizt. That all Taxes ought to originate with the people."[18]

In understanding the evolution in thinking of American popular leaders, an important factor is that these documents were created early in the year—before the British passed the Sugar Act of 1764 and revealed the intent to implement stamp duties. Bernard Bailyn has made the point that "in the overall development of the Revolutionary movement, these statements of colonial opinion, written before the passage of the Sugar Act, are of considerable importance."

> not only do they express the colonists' objections to the economic reorganization of the empire, but they mark the last point at which objections to Parliamentary action affecting them could generally be voiced without reference to ideology. The most striking fact about these addresses and petitions is their entire devotion to economic arguments: nowhere do they appeal to constitutional issues; nowhere was Parliament's right to pass such laws officially questioned.[19]

These protests made no complaint about control of trade by Great Britain, expecting the American grievance about the economic burden to be taken seriously by the mother country, and trusting that the colonies would not be economically harmed. The mild nature of the protests reflects that the Americans could not see that the British plans so far revealed were merely the first step in a policy change that was soon to be considered a manifest violation of their just and long-enjoyed rights.

PART TWO

Duties for Trade Regulation and Revenue

"Whereas it is expedient that new provisions and regulations should be established for *improving the revenue of this kingdom,* and for extending and *securing the navigation and commerce between* Great Britain and your Majesty's dominions in America . . . "

—The Sugar Act, April 5, 1764

Four

The Sugar Act of 1764

"A duty of 6d. per gallon upon molasses by the 6th of the late King was too heavy; this duty to be lowered therefore to 3d."
—George Grenville, March 9, 1764

"Whereas it is *just and necessary that a revenue be raised,* in your Majesty's said dominions in America . . . the commons of Great Britain, in parliament assembled . . . *have resolved to give and grant unto your Majesty* the several rates and duties herein-after-mentioned."
—The Sugar Act, April 5, 1764

IN APRIL 1774, EDMUND BURKE ADMONISHED THE HOUSE OF Commons for their impolitic action a decade earlier. "No act avowedly for the purpose of revenue," he said, "is found in the statute book until . . . the year 1764. All before this period stood on commercial regulation and restraint." The Sugar Act, the main vehicle for that change of policy, "opened *a new principle*: and here properly *began the second period of the policy of this country with regard to the colonies*; by which the scheme of a regular plantation parliamentary revenue was adopted in theory, and settled in practice." The change resulted in "perfect uncompensated slavery"[1] The First Continental Congress, writing in October 1774, expressed a sentiment similar to that of Burke regarding the change in policy. "The present unhappy situation of our affairs is occasioned by a *ruinous system of colony administration*, adopted by the British ministry about the year 1763."[2]

It is worth a pause to consider why Burke might have been so bold as to address the House of Commons in such a manner. We will hear much from him, and it is useful to establish his position in the British government. He was a member of the Rockingham faction in the House of Commons, becoming private secretary to Lord Rockingham in July 1765. Burke was elected a member later that year, and by 1774 was perhaps the most skilled debater in the house. Much of his extensive writing and speech-making was in defense of actions taken by the Rockingham administration of 1765-1766, and was consistently critical of the faction led by Grenville, especially his administration of 1764–1765. Burke was outstanding "for intellect, oratory, and drive," but lacked leadership qualities. As a politician he was unsuccessful, but "as a political theorist he was for posterity."[3] He was never an important decision-maker, but his speeches and writings provide insightful (if politically biased) analysis of important events in the story of the Sugar Act.

Although obvious in 1774, the situation was by no means clear a decade earlier. In addition to duties designed as both preferential tariffs and to raise revenue, the Sugar Act prescribes complex regulations intended to facilitate enforcement of the laws of trade. Particularly in this context, the duties seemed to be trade regulation, not a new principle at all, but rather long accepted as being within the rightful authority of Parliament.

HOW THE ACT CAME ABOUT

The story of how the Sugar Act of 1764 came about begins with the opening of Parliament in November 1763. The king's speech called for attention to "the heavy debts contracted in the course of the late war." He called for both frugality and "the improvement of the public revenue, by such regulations as shall be judged most expedient for that purpose."[4] Discussion about America was put aside for a few months to deal with pressing local matters, but on March 7, 1764, George Grenville announced that in two days "he would go at large into the ways and means," providing "some general idea of his plan, particularly as to the taxing of America."[5] The topic was not without controversy. "William Beckford at once raised what would become the central issue of the Stamp Act crisis, the constitutional role in this respect of 'the American legislatures.'"[6] (Beckford held large financial interests in the West Indies and—although in favor of the Sugar Act—was generally one of America's allies in opposition to taxation, opposing the Stamp Act in both 1764 and 1765.)

Grenville to the Committee of Ways and Means

On March 9, the British unveiled the policy change that had been brewing for over a year. Grenville presented to the committee of ways and means his budget proposals for the improvement of the public revenue. He dealt with British concern over American violation of the laws of trade and included resolutions that were the basis for duties of the Sugar Act of 1764; and since the new duties were not expected to raise adequate revenue, he included a resolution stating the need for an additional tax.[7]

After a long general introduction, including mention of Britain's "great debt," Grenville declares that it is time "to collect the Customs and prevent abuses by lowering the rate."

> This hour a very serious one. France in great distress at present, greater even than ours. Happy circumstance for us, as we are little able to afford another war, we have now peace; let us make the best use of it. Some remedies have opened themselves to us. The stationing ships has been of service.
>
> The House comes to the resolution to raise the revenue in America for defending itself. We have expended much in America. Let us now avail ourselves of the fruits of that expense. *The great object to reconcile the regulation of commerce with an increase of revenue.* With this view particularly desirable to prevent intercourse of America with foreign nations. And yet many colonies have such a trade. Such a trade has been opened by three or four colonies with France to the amount of £4 or 500,000 a year.

Grenville explains that preventing such American intercourse with foreign nations (in violation of the Navigation Acts) has already received great attention "by giving directions to the commissioners to prevent smuggling. This has been attended with success, the proportion from England has increased." (Forcing the trade to pass through British ports has a revenue aspect in that duties can be collected on such commerce.)

He then turns to the West Indies. "But this is not enough; you must collect the revenue from the plantations."

> First object would be to permit West Indian trade . . . To allow certain commodities from the French islands which are absolutely necessary, but to give preference to our own colonies' manufactures by paying duty upon the others.
>
> A duty of 6d. per gallon upon molasses by the 6th of the late King was too heavy; this duty to be lowered therefore to 3d. But the quantity so doubtful that he cannot form any certain estimate; perhaps £40, 50 or 60,000.

It is clear that the primary purpose of the molasses duty is to raise money; and even by the doubtful estimate provided by Grenville, it is expected to be an important source of revenue.

He quantifies the need for revenue. "Expense of maintaining 10,000 [British troops] in North America, amount £359,000."

There is a problem with ships carrying goods from Europe destined for America: specifically, ships that make the required stop in a British port but make false claims about the cargo. He describes the solution.

> That no ships shall be cleared out [for] North America unless shall unload all her goods *and take her clearance out for the whole and pay the duty for the whole.*

He next deals with wine imported into America. Wine imported to Great Britain for the purpose of re-export to America is to have a lower duty than previously. In addition, a new duty is to be placed on Madeira wine imported directly to America from wine-producing islands off the coast of Africa, often called the "Western Islands."

> Wines, to admit the wines from Portugal and Spain to go through with no other duty but the old subsidy of about £3.10.0, and a

small duty of 10s. upon its coming to North America. And to lay a duty on Madeira wine imported there.

Another problem has to do with illicit importation of foreign goods (especially sugar, rum, and molasses) from British plantations: fraudulent *naturalization* of foreign goods as being British, thereby avoiding duties. Grenville's solution is "to require a certificate that the goods coming from the [British] West Indian Islands are the produce of those islands."

He admits "the difficulty of executing these regulations." It is "difficult to find good officers who will go to North America. Smuggling therefore will continue and therefore, as this will diminish the revenue, *some further tax will be necessary* to defray the expense of North America." He then introduces stamp duties, a discussion that precipitates widespread American protest and resistance.[8]

Stamp duties the least exceptionable because it requires few officers and even collects itself. The only danger is forgery.

The related resolve is the soon-to-be controversial and eventually infamous fifteenth resolution (of twenty-four he introduced that day, all others dealing with the Sugar Act). There is no record of Grenville speaking the following specific words during his presentation, but it is useful to introduce them here. (We will later see the formal resolution.) *Towards further defraying the said Expences, it may be proper to charge certain Stamp Duties in the said Colonies and Plantations.* At this point, having heard rumblings to the contrary, Grenville wishes to affirm that Parliament holds the authority to impose such a tax on America.

He is convinced this country have the right to impose an inland tax. . . . If any man doubts the right of this country, he will take the opinion of a [the?] committee immediately.

No man doubted.

Grenville wraps up. "He owns the officers of the revenue must strike in the dark. However, he thinks this the best plan. He would likewise wish to follow to a certain degree the inclination of the people in North America if they will agree to the end."

Among the few to rise for discussion was Charles Jenkinson, who played such an important role in development of the Sugar Act. "He could easily confirm the right of England to impose taxes upon North America from Acts of Parliament and resolutions of the House of Commons."

John Huske, a native of New Hampshire who had resided in England for twenty-five years, had much to say. "Smugglers of molasses instead of being infamous are called patriots in North America. Nothing but a low duty can prevent it." He provides a small tutorial on molasses and reinforces the American claim that acquiring molasses is by barter for surplus North American products.

> Molasses duty has never brought in anything. French King has lately given our ships leave to take the molasses from his islands, which diminishes the expense per gallon of it, and therefore he approves of a duty of 2d. which he thinks much better than 3d., as there will be less temptation to smuggling. The molasses are bought off foreigners *by the superfluous lumber of our province and other things.*

Rum is vital to American commerce. "30 ships go from New England every year laden with nothing but rum, and bring back gold dust, elephants' teeth and slaves for the sugar planters." He supports the standard colonial argument that "the more North America gets, the more it will be able to remit to us for manufactures." Then he provides a negative analysis of the three pence duty. "A duty on molasses at 2d per gallon will yield about £58,000; at 3d it will not produce £25,000."

Grenville spoke again, perhaps responding to suggestions that the stamp duties be postponed. "As to stamp duty, desired it might be done with good will. That for the present session it might go no farther than a resolution." The fact that he proposed stamp duties in 1764 but postponed the Stamp Act until 1765 is part of the story of the Sugar Act; the American protests of 1764 were often muddled by the mixing of constitutional objections to the use of stamp duties with commercial objections to the Sugar Act.[9]

Passage of the Act

On March 10, the committee of ways and means reported twenty-four resolutions to the full House, all eventually approved.[10] They include, "[15] That, towards further defraying the said Expences, it may be proper to charge certain Stamp Duties in the said Colonies and Plantations." It was ordered, "That a Bill, or Bills, be brought in pursuant to [all resolutions save the fifteenth]."

On March 12, the house ordered those who were preparing the bills to include regulations necessary for its enforcement.

> That they do make Provision in the said Bill, or in One of the said Bills, for more effectually preventing the clandestine Exportation, Importation, and Conveyance of Goods to and from the British Colonies and Plantations in America; and for improving and securing the Trade between Great Britain and the said Colonies and Plantations.

The order was in response to a Grenville call for procedures that would allow customs officers to determine what a vessel was carrying, the destination of the cargo, and where it had previously called. In addition, the act was to allow prosecution in courts of admiralty, avoiding the juries in common-law courts that had in the past been so quick to acquit accused smugglers. The result was the addition of a number of sections that define regulatory processes and procedures intended to provide for effective enforcement of the laws of trade.

On March 22, there was debate regarding further lowering the duty on molasses, but Grenville prevailed at three pence. Other issues were later debated as well, but there was no significant change; and there was no attempt to present American objections. The resulting bill was approved by the Commons on March 30, sent up to the Lords, and passed (without debate) on April 4. It received the royal assent on April 5, 1764.

When the king put an end to the session of Parliament on April 19, he included these words of praise for the House of Commons.

> The wise regulations which have been established to augment the public revenues, to unite the interests of the most distant posses-

sions of my crown, and to encourage and secure their commerce with Great Britain, call for my hearty approbation.[11]

Justification

Before introducing the text of the act, it is useful to look at a justification for the duties and regulations imposed. The most important analysis, including description and rationale for specific provisions of the act, is contained in a 114-page pamphlet: *The Regulations Lately Made*. It was written by Thomas Whately (a principal secretary in the Treasury and a particularly close confidante and spokesman for Grenville). Initially published anonymously in January 1765, and at first thought to be written by Grenville himself, it was little short of an official statement of the government, serving as an explanation and defense of actions taken by Parliament in 1764.[12]

> The Commercial Interests of Great Britain, are now preferred to every other Consideration: And the Trade from whence its greatest Wealth is derived, and upon which its Maritime Power is principally founded, depends upon a *wise and proper use of the Colonies*.

His explanation of wise and proper use repeats the classic rationale for having colonies: that they must provide raw materials to, and in turn, consume the manufactures of, the "Mother-Country."

After a long dissertation about the value of the Navigation Acts, Whately eventually turns to the Sugar Act. The Americans have grown to become an "opulent, commercial, thriving people," made so by British protection and policies: "supported by her Wealth, protected by her Power, and blessed with her Laws." Therefore, "there is no Occasion to accompany this Account with any Observations; only to state it, is to prove the Necessity of an additional American Revenue; they can certainly bear more; they ought to raise more." He describes the genesis of the Sugar Act.

> It came under the Deliberation of Parliament the last Winter 1764, and by their Wisdom an Act was passed to be the Foundation of an American Revenue, which is formed upon such Principles, that

the Increase in the Revenue, which may be expected from it, tho' very considerable, *seems the least important Object*; so very judicious, so very interesting are the several Provisions of this Act, for the Purposes of *Commerce and Colonization.*

He may think revenue the "least important Object," but the duties being imposed for revenue were (not initially, but by 1774) the primary grievance raised by the Americans.

Here is a general rationale for duties and prohibitions.

To encourage the Consumption of our own Produce and our own Manufactures, in preference to those of other Countries, has been at all times an undisputed Maxim of Policy; and for this Purpose, high Duties and even Prohibitions have been laid Upon foreign Commodities, while Bounties have been granted on our own. The general Tendency of the Act now before us is to extend the same Principle to the American, as is followed in respect to our home Trade and Consumption.

Annual British exports to America are of value £1.4 million, including foreign goods legally passing through British ports in accordance with the Navigation Acts.

Goods imported annually from Great Britain into America, amount in Value to the Sum of 1,400,000*l.* and that one Third of these are foreign Goods re-exported from hence.

In addition to the legal re-exported goods, "it is commonly supposed that foreign Goods to the Amount of 700,000*l.* are annually smuggled into the Colonies." (Referring to European trade, not the West Indies.)

Should the Regulations, I shall presently mention, to have been made for the Prevention of all illicit Trade, have the Effect that is to be wished, to bring the greater Part of these too in the regular Channel thro' Great Britain, in which Case [duties would be paid] then the Amount of this Duty upon all, will really be considerable.

He reinforces the idea that the duties imposed in 1764 were intended not only for revenue, but for strengthening the relationship with America.

The several Duties imposed by Parliament . . . appear to have been *judiciously chosen, not only with a View* to the Revenue, which they will produce; but for other, and in my Opinion, greater political Purposes; [including enhancing] *the Trade of Great Britain, and* [the] *Connection between her and her Colonies*; tho' the Duties are very low, the Articles on which they are laid are numerous, and comprehend all that have been the Subjects of a contraband Trade, with those Parts of Europe which the Colonies are not allowed to trade to. The bringing these to a regular Entry and Account, will be the Means of detecting and of preventing the illicit Proceedings that have hitherto prevailed.

Further, he observes, "In other Countries Custom-house Duties are for the most Part, little more than a Branch of the Revenue." Here, the situation is different.

In the Colonies they are a political Regulation, and enforce the Observance of those wise Laws to which the great Increase of our Trade and naval Power are principally owing. *The Aim of those Laws is to confine the European Commerce of the Colonies to the Mother Country*: to provide that their most valuable Commodities shall be exported either to Great Britain or to British Plantations; and to secure the Navigation of all American Exports and Imports to British Ships and British Subjects only.[13]

As a final step before going into detail about the text of the Sugar Act, it is useful to summarize the most important goods upon which duties are placed. (Foreign rum is prohibited.) By and large, the duties are levied as preferential tariffs in addition to being expected to raise revenue.

1. Foreign molasses. In contrast, British molasses is duty-free.

2. Foreign sugar. The duty is higher than the existing export duties on British West Indies sugar.

3. Wine imported directly from Madeira and the Azores, the

"Western Islands." Previously duty-free, the duties are higher than those levied on wine imported from Great Britain.

4. Wine imported from Great Britain. Such wine being that re-exported from European sources (including from the Western Islands).

5. Foreign coffee. It bears a heavy duty in comparison to a modest duty on British-grown coffee.

6. British coffee. Although the duty is low, it serves no purpose of trade regulation; it is imposed strictly for revenue.

TEXT OF THE ACT

The Sugar Act of 1764 (4 George III c. 15)[14] renewed and amended the Sugar Act of 1733.

The title:

An act for granting certain duties in the British colonies and plantations in America; *for continuing, amending, and making perpetual* [the Sugar Act of 1733]; for applying the produce of such duties . . . towards defraying the expences of defending, protecting, and securing the said colonies and plantations . . . and more effectually preventing the clandestine conveyance of goods to and from the said colonies and plantations, and *improving and securing the trade* between the same and Great Britain.

The preamble:

Whereas it is expedient that new provisions and regulations should be established for *improving the revenue* of this kingdom, and for extending and securing the navigation and commerce between Great Britain and your Majesty's dominions in America, which, by the peace, have been so happily enlarged; and whereas it is *just and necessary that a revenue be raised*, in your Majesty's said dominions in America, for defraying the expenses of defending, protecting, and securing the same; we, your Majesty's most dutiful and loyal subjects, the commons of Great Britain, in parliament assembled, being desirous to make some provision, in this present session of parliament, towards raising the said revenue in America, have *resolved to give and grant unto your Majesty* the several rates and duties herein-after-mentioned.

There are phrases in both title and preamble that are regulation of trade: "improving and securing the trade," and "extending and securing the navigation and commerce." As a consequence—and particularly since the title makes it clear the act is a continuation of the trade regulation of 1733—Americans did not at first recognize it as an act of taxation; there was good reason for such a viewpoint. The bulk of the act has to do with documentation of cargoes and rules for the control of trade, and the duties are levied largely in the form of preferential tariffs. There is certainly nothing that shouts, "This is taxation!" On the other hand, the preamble does contain important phrases that signal a money bill: "improving the revenue" and "that a revenue be raised." It grants duties and appropriates them to a specific purpose; and it repeats the "give and grant" words of donation. (In fact, the Sugar Act of 1764 is the first act dealing with America that includes both words of donation and additional words of art that a revenue should be raised.) In short, the act was designed to both raise revenue and to regulate trade.

The preamble continues that, after September 29, 1764, "there shall be raised, levied, collected, and paid . . . for and upon [a list of foreign goods] which shall be imported or brought into any [British] colony or plantation in America . . . the several rates and duties following;"

> For every hundred weight avoirdupois of such foreign white or clayed sugars, one pound two shillings, over and above all other duties imposed by any former act of parliament.

The rate on such sugars imposed in 1733 was 5s, the same as the export duty on British white sugar. In sum, the duty on foreign white or clayed sugars becomes £1 7s, while that on brown sugar remains unchanged at 5s (still higher than the export duty on British brown sugar at 1s 6d).

Whately points out that the sugar duty "cannot be complained of by the Americans, so far as their own Consumption is affected by it, since the Inhabitants of Great Britain have chearfully submitted their Consumption to the like Regulation, and for the Benefit of the West India Plantations, have laid a *much higher Duty upon French than upon British* Sugars imported into Great Britain."[15]

The act places a very high duty on foreign coffee, almost £3 per hundredweight, intended as a preferential tariff in favor of coffee from the British islands.

> For every hundred weight avoirdupois of such foreign coffee, which shall be imported from any place, except Great Britain, two pounds, nineteen shillings, and nine pence.

Much more important than foreign coffee from a revenue point of view is this high duty of £7 per ton on wine from the Western Islands. (Before the Sugar Act, most wine imported into America was duty-free Madeira wine laden in the Azores.)

> For every ton of wine of the growth of the Madeiras, or of any other island or place from whence such wine may be lawfully imported, and which shall be so imported from such islands or place, the sum of seven pounds.

(The high import duty also hampered the export of surplus American products such as wheat, flour, fish, and lumber.) The same wine imported via a British port carried a lower duty.

> For every ton of Portugal, Spanish, or any other wine (except French wine) *imported from Great Britain*, the sum of ten shillings.[16]

This low import duty was in addition to duties levied in Great Britain explained in section 12.

Sections 2 and 3 address British coffee.[17]

> II. And it is hereby further enacted . . . [duties to be paid] for and upon all coffee . . . of the growth and produce of any British colony or plantation in America, which shall be there laden on board any British ship or vessel, to be carried out from thence to any other place whatsoever, except Great Britain [the following duty].

The phrase "shall be there laden on board" makes this an export duty, but in practice was collected at the port of importation.

III. For every hundred weight avoirdupois of such British coffee, seven shillings.

The low duty is intended to provide "an advantage over that pro-duced in foreign Plantations." As a consequence, "so great a Differ-ence of Duty . . . must give a Preference to our own Produce."[18] Coffee makes for a good example of a mix of taxation and trade reg-ulation. While the duty levied on British coffee is much lower than that on foreign coffee, there is no trade rationale for placing any duty at all on British coffee; the only purpose of such a duty is to raise revenue. Although clearly a tax, since the burden was small this cof-fee tax never became a noteworthy grievance of the Americans.

In section 4, the 1733 act, which was about to expire, is continued one more time "in order that all persons concerned may have due and proper notice thereof." In section 5, "the said act, subject to such alterations and amendments as are herein after contained, shall be, and the same is hereby made perpetual."

The most forceful American protests of early 1764 (chapter 3) were to the rate of duty on foreign molasses. Section 6 reduces that duty. It is primarily intended to produce revenue, but retains the pre-tense of being a preferential tariff compared to duty-free British mo-lasses.

VI. In lieu and instead of the rate and duty imposed by the said act [Sugar Act of 1733] upon molasses and syrups, there shall . . . be raised, levied, collected, and paid, unto his Majesty, his heirs and successors, for and upon every gallon of [foreign] molasses or syrups . . . which shall be imported or brought into any colony or plantation in America, which now is, or hereafter may be, under the dominion of his Majesty, his heirs or successors, *the sum of three pence.*

Whately justifies the three pence duty (which the Americans thought still too high, even prohibitive) with a complex argument re-lated to increased enforcement (hence increased cost for clandestine trade) allowing for a higher duty. He also argues that since "a Gallon of Melasses produces a Gallon of Rum," the extra duty is particularly easy to absorb given the high demand for rum, and its insensitivity to price. Whately goes on for page after page about molasses, including belittling American objections to the high rate. "Something more than mere Apprehensions and general Assertions are necessary to condemn a Tax which appears so proper on so many Accounts; and unless Experience should prove that it is attended with bad Consequences [and on and on]." In any event, it was the rate judged by Grenville that would maximize revenue. Combined with the continuing pretense of a preferential tariff, it was a dual-purpose duty: revenue and trade regulation.

Whately further claims that the French can be forced to pay whatever is necessary to compensate for the three pence duty on molasses; the French depend upon North America "for the Subsistance of their Inhabitants . . . as they can no where else procure in any Quantity, or at any tolerable Price, the Casks and other Material that are necessary for [their commerce]. . . . They cannot refuse our Provisions and our Lumber." Furthermore, they are more dependent now after the war since French dominions on the continent have been ceded to Great Britain.[19]

Section 7 incorporates the 1733 Sugar Act and the 1673 Plantation Act.

> VII. The said rates and duties . . . shall be raised, levied, collected, and paid, in the same manner and form [and so on, as in the act of 1733 and the act of 1673]; and that all powers, penalties, provisions, articles, and clauses, in those acts [apply] as fully and *effectually as if the same were particularly and at large re-enacted in the body of this present act.*

Sections 8 through 10 establish various additional detailed regulations. Section 11 dictates how funds are allocated to "his Majesty's Exchequer" and appropriates the revenue to support a British army in America.

> XI. And it is hereby further enacted . . . that all the monies which . . . shall arise by the several rates and duties herein before granted; and also [duties on sugar levied in the 1733 act] shall be paid into

the receipt of his Majesty's Exchequer, and shall be entered separate and apart from all other monies paid . . . and shall be there
reserved to be, from time to time, disposed of by parliament, towards defraying the necessary expences of defending, protecting,
and securing, the British colonies and plantations in America.

The explicit appropriation is particularly important since the duties were to be collected in sterling money. Some Americans later
protested that the act would remove hard currency from America;
this was incorrect, at least after the money was expended in America.
A spokesman for the ministry later admitted that "the order to send
all the money arising from these duties to his Majesty's Exchequer in
England was a very imprudent move."[20]

Section 12 changes the refund paid for duties on wine imported
to Great Britain for re-export to America, reducing the effective duty
for such wines to £3 10s. per ton.

XII. . . . upon the exportation of any sort of wine (except French
wines) from this kingdom to any British colony or plantation in
America, as merchandize, the exporter shall be paid, in lieu of all
former drawbacks, a drawback or allowance of all the duties paid
upon the importation of such wine, except the sum of three
pounds ten shillings per ton.

Adding the 10s import duty collected in the colonies (as levied in
the preamble), not so much for revenue wrote Whately, as "to make
the respective Custom-house Accounts, checks upon each other,"
makes for a total duty of £4 as imported into the colonies.[21] This
duty is important in comparison to the duty of £7 on wine imported
directly from the Western Islands. Despite the £3 difference in the
rate of duty, the extra expense and travel time to import such wine
via Great Britain (and the need to export American goods) was such
that much wine continued to be imported directly from the islands,
merchants paying the duty of £7 per ton.

The duty on wine was not a trade regulation; it was a tax. The
First Continental Congress dealt with this issue on October 21, 1774,
in the *Address to the People of Great Britain*. "Although no wine is

made in any country subject to the British state, you prohibited our procuring it of foreigners without paying a tax imposed by your Parliament on all we imported. These and many other impositions were laid upon us most unjustly and unconstitutionally for the express purpose of raising a revenue."[22]

Section 18 prohibits importation of foreign rum, reducing competition both for British rum and locally distilled rum in the colonies.

> XVIII. No rum or spirits of the produce or manufacture of any of the [foreign islands] shall be imported or brought into any of the [British] colonies or plantations in America.

French sugar planters are forbidden by French regulations to produce rum for domestic use ("as it affects the Consumption of her Brandy") but will produce it for export when possible. Such production takes jobs away from Americans in the distillery industry; therefore, the prohibition of rum is established "in order to force the French to supply the Demands of our Colonies for their Molasses."[23]

The act contains additional sections, forty-seven in total, defining regulatory processes and procedures intended to provide for effective enforcement of the laws of trade.[24]

Section 20 is intended to ensure that sugar, rum, and molasses from British plantations is precisely identified. It is a tedious procedure, designed to prevent illicit naturalization of those foreign products. Let's first look at Whately's summary explanation. "For the further Prevention of the Smuggling of foreign Rum, Sugars, and Melasses, which are *great Objects of clandestine Trade*, it is provided, that whenever any of those Commodities are shipped, as the Growth of a British Plantation, it shall be proved upon Oath that they are so; and a *Certificate of such Oath* having been taken, shall be given to the Master of the Vessel, who must produce it at the Port of Delivery."[25]

> XX. For the better preventing frauds in the importation of foreign sugars and paneles, rum and spirits, molasses and syrups, into any of his Majesty's dominions, under pretence that the same are the growth, produce, or manufacture, of the British colonies or plan-

tations . . . every person or persons loading on board any ship or vessel, in any of the British colonies or plantations in America, any rum [or sugar or molasses] as of the growth, product, or manufacture, of any British colony or plantation, shall, *before the clearing out* of the said ship or vessel, produce and *deliver to the collector* or other principal officer of the customs at the loading port, an affidavit signed and sworn to before some justice of the peace in the said British colonies or plantation.

(The *collector* plays a central role in enforcement, and is often featured, along with "or other principal officer of the customs" in the regulations prescribed by the Sugar Act.) The sworn affidavit is to be from "the grower, maker, or shipper, of such goods [expressing] the quality of the goods so shipped, with the number and denomination of the packages, and describing the name or names of the plantation or plantations, and the name of the colony where the same grew or were produced and manufactured."

The collector . . . to whom such affidavit shall be delivered, shall thereupon grant to the master, or other person having the charge of the ship or vessel, *a certificate* under his hand and seal of office [restating the information in the sworn affidavit].

The collector is required to "transmit an exact copy of the said affidavit to the secretary's office for the respective colony or plantation where the goods were shipped." The final step is a cross-check of one document upon another.

XXI. And it is further enacted, That upon the arrival of such ship or vessel into the port of her discharge, either in Great Britain or any other port of his Majesty's dominions, where such goods may be lawfully imported, the master or other person taking the charge of the ship or vessel shall . . . *deliver the said certificate* to the collector . . . and make oath before him, that the goods so reported are the same that are mentioned in the said certificate.

Section 23 deals at length with the specific problem of illicit import of molasses taken as return cargo from foreign colonies. Although a burden on merchants (one of the most trying regulations of the act), it is in effect for only two years, superseded by new regulations established in 1766. It starts by restating existing bond requirements for *enumerated* goods, and Whately is satisfied that "the Parties concerned obliged themselves to comply with the Laws that relate to them." However, "when *non-enumerated* Goods only have been shipped, no Security has ever been taken for the proper Disposal of the Returns usually made from the foreign Plantations [thereby allowing] great Quantities of foreign Melasses and Syrups [to be] clandestinely run into the Colonies."[26]

The act states it this way:

XXIII. . . . great quantities of foreign molasses and syrups are clandestinely run on shore in the British colonies [i.e., North America] to the prejudice of the revenue, and the great detriment of the trade of this kingdom and it's American plantations [i.e., in the British West Indies];

The remedy is to require that bond must be given

at any port or place in any of the British American colonies or plantations [for] *every ship or vessel* that shall lade or take on board there any goods not *particularly enumerated* in the said acts, being the product or manufacture of any of the said colonies or plantations, with condition, that, *in case any molasses or syrups*, being the produce of [foreign colonies] shall be laden on board such ship or vessel [i.e., as return cargo], the same shall [be brought] to some of his Majesty's colonies or plantations in America, or to some port in Great Britain; and that the master or other person having the charge of such ship or vessel, shall, immediately upon his arrival . . . make a just and true report of all the goods laden on board.

The rationale for that remedy as expressed by Whately is that importers would be deterred from attempting to smuggle if they were subject "to Penalties of their Bonds upon Detection." He summarizes the effect of the provision as "a Bond therefore is by this Act required on the loading of *non-enumerated* Goods also, *with Condition, that if* any foreign Melasses or Syrups shall be taken on board in Return the same shall be brought to Great Britain, or to a British Plantation."[27] The vexing problem for merchants is that bonds are henceforth required for shipping non-enumerated products: lumber, horses, beef, fish, wheat, and on and on; and the bonds are required *for every ship or vessel*, any size, decked or undecked, even for coastal traffic within the same colony.

Section 24 deals with certificates to be given at the port of lading certifying that bonds have been given. Whately explains. "But whether Bond had been given in either of these Cases [enumerated or not] . . . could not be known at any other Place than the Port from whence the Vessel departed." Therefore, the new regulation is that the "Master of such Vessel [is now] obliged to take out a Certificate of his having complied with the Law."[28]

> XXIV. Every master or person having the charge of *any ship or vessel* shall, before he departs from any British colony or plantation *where he receives his lading*, take a certificate under the hands and seals of the collector . . . that bond hath been given, pursuant to the directions of this or any other act of parliament [and] shall keep such certificate in his custody till the voyage is compleated, and shall then deliver the same up to the collector . . . at the port or *place where he shall discharge his lading*.

Section 25 establishes a requirement to show documentation.

> XXV. If any British ship or vessel laden, as aforesaid, with any goods of the produce or manufacture of any British colony or plantation in America, or having on board any molasses or syrups the produce of any foreign colony or plantation, shall be discovered by any officer of his Majesty's customs within two leagues of the shore of any British colony or plantation in America, and the master or person taking charge of such ship or vessel shall not produce a certificate that bond has been given . . . or if he shall not produce such certificate to the collector . . . where he shall arrive [the ship and goods are subject to seizure and prosecution].

For vessels at sea, the "discovery" would typically be made by the

Royal Navy, leading to another American grievance. "The empowering commanders of the King's ships to seize and implead, as is done in this act and a former act [i.e., Hovering Act] and by special commission from the commissioners of the customs, is another great hardship on the colonies. The knowledge of all the statutes relating to the customs, of all the prohibitions on exports and imports, and of various intricate cases arising on them, requires a good lawyer. How can this science ever be expected from men educated in a totally different way, brought up upon the boisterous element and knowing no law aboard their ships but their own will?"[29]

Sections 27 and 28 add more destination restrictions on specific products. Whately explains. "The Policy of prohibiting certain enumerated Goods, from being exported out of the Plantations, except to some other British Plantation, or to Great Britain, was introduced by the first Act of Trade and Navigation, and has been adopted in many subsequent Statutes." He gives some rationale and then explains that a number of goods "are by the Act of the last Sessions added to the enumerated Commodities."[30]

> XXVII. All coffee, pimento, cocoa nuts, whale fins, raw silks, hides and skins, pot[ash] and pearl ashes, of the growth, production, or manufacture, of any British colony or plantation in America, *shall be imported* directly from thence into this kingdom, or some other British colony or plantation.

A lesser restriction on iron and lumber allows them still to be carried to the foreign plantations in the West Indies. "Iron and Lumber, tho' of equal Utility, yet being a great Article of Trade in foreign Plantations, are allowed to be disposed of there."[31]

> XXVIII. No iron, nor any sort of wood, commonly called Lumber . . . of the growth, production, or manufacture, of any British colony or plantation in America, shall be there loaden on board any ship or vessel to be carried from thence, until sufficient bond . . . shall be given . . . that the said goods shall not be landed in any part of Europe except Great Britain.

This provision disrupted an existing trade route with Ireland. Benjamin Franklin, writing Richard Jackson on June 25, explains the problem.

> The Thing in it I least understand the Policy of, is your forbidding us to carry Iron and Lumber directly to Ireland. Flaxseed we carry thither in great Quantities, and Staves [lumber] us'd to be pack'd between the Casks, with some Pig Iron at the Bottom for Ballast. The Staves are a trifling Commodity, and the Quantity small in such a Cargo; and it cannot be worth while for the sake of carrying them, to enter first and unload in England; and we do not see how that Trade could hurt or affect any Interest of Britain.[32]

The next year, 5 George III c. 45 (May 22, 1765) repealed these restrictions as far as importation into Ireland was concerned. Specifically, "extend the importation of such iron, and also to extend the importation of such wood, commonly called Lumber, to Ireland."[33]

Whately next (as does the Sugar Act text at this point) shifts his attention to the need to restrict American coastal traffic as an aid to the prevention of illicit importation of foreign goods. Whately points out that it is not sufficient to simply have "Guards against clandestine Importations." Illicit goods that evaded such guards "would be to a Degree in Safety as soon as they were landed, and might be carried out again along the neighboring Coasts with Security, if the Vigilance of the Law stopped here."[34]

Section 29 expands the control over intercolonial trade instituted by the Plantation Act of 1673 (which established control only over enumerated goods). Henceforth, all intercolonial trade is to be subject to detailed regulation through a system of permissions and cockets. This provision placed a crippling burden on the master of a vessel—any vessel, any size, decked or undecked, regardless of what sort of goods were being shipped, and even if only intended for river trade from one colony to another.

First, the purpose:

> XXIX. For the better preventing frauds in the importation or exportation of goods that are liable to the payment of duties, or are

prohibited, in the British colonies or plantations in America, it is further enacted . . .

Here is the requirement that, *before loading any goods aboard his ship*, the master must obtain authorization from a customs officer.

> No goods, wares, or merchandizes, *of any kind whatsoever*, shall be shipped or laden on board *any ship or vessel* in any of the British colonies or plantations in America, to be carried from thence *to any other British colony* or plantation, without a sufferance or warrant first had and obtained from the collector . . . at the port or place where such goods shall be intended to be put on board.

Obtaining authorization before loading, taken literally, would put a stop to much intercolonial trade. The problem, other than at major ports with covered storage, is that farmers or merchants might arrive intermittently with cargo that cannot remain in the open. Even worse, a ship might go from place to place to load cargo. In the past, ships would load cargo as convenient, afterward dealing with customs procedures.[35]

In addition, there is a new requirement for cockets, issued by customs officers.

> The master of *every such ship or vessel* shall, before the same be removed or carried out from the port or place where he takes in his lading, take out a cocket or cockets expressing the quantity and quality of the goods, and marks of the package, so laden, with the merchants names by whom shipped and to whom consigned; and if they are goods that liable to the payment of any duty, either upon the importation into, or upon the exportation from, the said colonies or plantation, the said cocket or cockets shall likewise distinctly specify that the duties have been paid for the same, referring to the times or dates of entry and payment of such duties, and by whom they were paid;

Cockets were needed at the port of arrival.

which cocket or cockets shall be produced by the master of such ship or vessel, to the collector . . . at the port of place where such ship or vessel shall arrive in any of the British colonies or plantations in America, before any part of the goods are unladen or put on shore.

Further:

Any officer of his Majesty's customs is hereby empowered to stop any such ship or vessel, bound aforesaid, which shall be discovered within two leagues of the shore of any of the said British colonies.

Whately describes the effect (the beneficial effect for Great Britain) in this manner. "The Danger [to smugglers] therefore of an illicit Commerce is continued beyond the first Importation, and the Vent of smuggled Goods is laid under still further Difficulties and Discouragements; for *no Merchandize whatever can now be conveyed by Sea from one Colony to another*, without a Sufferance, upon which a Cocket is to be made out, particularly specifying the Goods, and the Duties that have been paid thereon."[36] A particularly vexing aspect of this act is that naval officers serving as customs officials interpreted the phrase "such ship" (with, as Whately put it, "Merchandize . . . conveyed by Sea") as meaning *any waterborne vessel*, thereby interpreting this regulation as including river traffic.

As an illustration of the American problem with these restrictions, here is a complaint from the chief justice of Pennsylvania, writing to Barclay & Sons in London on November 20, 1764.

No doubt you will hear fully of the low Ebb of Trade, which is distressed exceedingly; even the Intercourse between here [Philadelphia] & New Jersey is, in a great Measure interrupted, which was carried on in Flats & small Boats, and the Produce of the Western part of that Colony shipped oft from this City, But now, one of those poor fellows cannot take in a few Staves, or Pig Iron, or Bar Iron, or Tar &c, but they must go thirty or forty Miles, or more to give Bond, *the Charge of which & his travelling, make the Burthen intolerable.*

The chief justice makes the assertion that "*it never was the Intention of the Legislature at home to destroy this little River-Trade, which is carried on in a kind of Market Boats, but their Emulations were only for Sea Vessels.*"

> This is a general Complaint all over the Continent; Such Measures will soon make us poor, but our Creditors in England will suffer with us. We must learn Frugality and make all our necessaries ourselves, for we shall soon not be able to get them any other way, as our Money is gone, and our Credit will soon be at an end.[37]

The restrictions were so troublesome that Parliament acted to correct the problem. On May 10, 1765, Whately wrote that "a bill is now before ye House which relates almost entirely to the colonies. *It is intended to remove all reasonable objections to the act of last year*; to allow the passage of all vessels without decks within a certain distance of the shore & under certain descriptions" to not be subject to such strict regulations.[38] Let's look further at that act (which we saw earlier), 5 George III c. 45.[39] Since requiring cockets for goods

> which are not liable to any duty by any act of Parliament . . . *may lay an unnecessary restraint upon the trade and correspondence of his Majesty's American subjects*, when such goods are carried merely for the use and sustenance of the said colonies, in boats or small vessels without decks which do not go to open sea; . . . the said recited act shall not extend, [to] any boat, flat, shallop, or other *vessel without a deck*, not exceeding twenty tons burthen, and shall be carried within any river, lake, or other inland waters, within the said colonies or plantations, and shall not be carried out to sea farther than one league from the shore.[40]

Edmund Burke, in 1769, used this regulation and its correction to attack the Grenville party; he wrote of Grenville's excessive keenness for regulation. "Some of [the new regulations] the ministry which gave them birth was obliged to destroy; with their own hand they signed the condemnation of their own regulations, confessing in so many words, in the preamble of their act of the 5th Geo. III., that some of these regulations had laid an *unnecessary restraint on the trade and correspondence* of his Majesty's American subjects. This, in that ministry, was a candid confession of a mistake." More broadly, Burke rebuked Grenville for "the multiplicity and intricacy of regulations and ordinances" that embarrassed the trade of America. Grenville "seemed to be possessed with something, hardly short of a rage, for regulation and restriction. He had so multiplied bonds, certificates, affidavits, warrants, sufferances, and cockets; had supported them with such severe penalties, and extended them without the least consideration of circumstances to so many objects, that, had they all continued in their original force, commerce must speedily have expired under them."[41]

For section 30, it is helpful to first listen to Whately. "The Attention of the Legislature has not however been confined to America. Frauds practiced in Britain with a View to a clandestine Trade in the Colonies, have fallen under their Notice; and to prevent them it has been found necessary to regulate the Trade from hence to the Colonies. It has been a common practice for British Ships provided with a Cargo in foreign Countries, which was pretended to be destined for a foreign Plantation, just to touch at some Out-port of this Kingdom, and there to take small Parcels of Goods on board, which they entered for a British colony. Under cover of these, however inconsiderable, they gained Admittance into the American Ports, and there, Opportunities were not wanting to run the whole Cargoes on shore."[42] First, the situation, formally stated.

> XXX. Whereas British vessels arriving from foreign parts at several of the out ports of this kingdom, fully or in part laden abroad with goods that *are pretended to be destined to some foreign plantation*, do frequently take on board some small parcels of goods in this kingdom which are entered outwards for some British colony or plantation, and a cocket and clearance thereupon granted for such goods,

Here is the problem, and the solution:

> under cover of which the whole cargoes of such vessels are *clandestinely landed in the British American dominions*, contrary to

several acts of parliament now in force, to the great prejudice of the trade and revenue of the kingdom; for remedy whereof . . . no ship or vessel shall, upon any pretence whatsoever, be cleared outwards from any port of this kingdom, for any land, island, plantation, colony, territory, or place, to his Majesty belonging . . . in America, unless *the whole and entire cargo* of such ship or vessel shall be bona fide, and without fraud, laden and shipped in this kingdom;

In other words, any such ship must be unloaded and reloaded under the supervision of customs officers. (As Grenville phrased it during his budget proposals, "shall unload all her goods and take her clearance out for the whole and pay the duty for the whole.") Each ship must at that point obtain "a cocket or clearance from the collector . . . certifying that the said goods were laden on board the said ship or vessel in some port of Great Britain." For enforcement,

any officer of his Majesty's customs is hereby empowered to stop any British ship or vessel arriving from any part of Europe, which shall be discovered within two leagues of the shore of any of the said British colonies or plantations in America.

Whately explains how section 30 defeats the "pernicious Contrivance" of using small parcels of goods to access American ports. "No Ship can from henceforth be cleared out from any British Port for any American Port, unless her whole Cargo be laden here; and all Goods which shall he found on board, and which are not expressly described in the Cocket which the Master is obliged to take, are liable to be seized."

Whately diverges at this point from the text of the Sugar Act. His meander gives some insight into the thinking of British leaders, and demonstrates that there is more to the Sugar Act than can be seen simply by study of the text. Whately points out that these regulations not only contribute to "the Prevention of Smuggling . . . to the Improvement of the Revenue, and to the Regulation of Commerce," they at the same time enhance "the great Purpose of supporting a naval Power" by keeping "a Body of Seamen fit for Service," adding that "they will not be Seamen long, if active Business is not found for them." As part of a longer rationale, he notes that "the Officers and the Men who are engaged in this Duty are encouraged to perform it with Spirit and Alacrity by the Prizes they may expect."[43]

Section 32 establishes a penalty for alteration of documents: "counterfeit, raise, alter, or falsify, any affidavit, certificate, sufferance, cocket, or clearance." Section 33 establishes a penalty in the case a customs officer should "directly or indirectly, take or receive any bribe . . . or connive at any false entry."

Governors are required to take an oath that they will be diligent in their duty.

> XXXIX. Governors or commanders in chief of any British colony or plantation shall . . . take a solemn oath, to do their utmost that all the clauses, matters, and things, contained in any act of parliament heretofore made, and now in force, relating to the said colonies and plantations, and that all and every the clauses contained in this present act, be punctually and bona fide observed, according to the true intent and meaning thereof.

The act specifies "penalties, forfeitures, and disabilities, either for neglecting to take the said oath, or for wittingly neglecting to do their duty accordingly." (This requirement reinforces trade instructions routinely given by the king to newly appointed governors.)

Section 41, first of all, requires that payment of duties be in hard currency.

> XLI. All sums of money granted and imposed by this act . . . as rates or duties; and also all sums of money imposed as penalties or forfeitures . . . shall be [paid in] sterling money of Great Britain,

Second, it allows for prosecution in courts of admiralty.

> . . . and that all the forfeitures and penalties *inflicted by this or any other act or acts of parliament relating to the trade and revenues* of the said British colonies or plantations in America [i.e., the acts of trade], which shall be incurred there, shall and may be prosecuted, sued for, and recovered in any court of record [i.e., a

common-law court], or in any court of admiralty, in the said colonies or plantations where such offence shall be committed, or in any court of vice admiralty which may or shall be appointed over all America (which court of admiralty or vice admiralty are hereby respectively authorized and required to proceed, hear, and determine the same) at the *election of the informer or prosecutor.*

The Sugar Act of 1733 similarly allowed prosecution in admiralty courts at the option of the prosecutor, but this enlarged the scope of such courts beyond maritime offenses.[44] Every serious American protest of 1764 and 1765 included the admiralty court as a grievance, always objecting to the unconstitutional nature of such courts. The First Continental Congress in 1774 addressed the use of admiralty courts, "by which means the subject lost the advantage of being tried by an honest uninfluenced jury of the vicinage, and was subjected to the sad necessity of being judged by a single man, a creature of the crown." In addition, the act of 1764 set up different rules in Great Britain and America. In England "the penalties and forfeitures *incurred there*, are to be recovered in any of the King's Courts of Record [whereas in America] the penalties and forfeitures *incurred here*, are to be recovered in any Court of Record, or in any court of Admiralty, or Vice-Admiralty at the election of the informer or prosecutor."[45]

Oxenbridge Thacher, an essayist and important legislator in Massachusetts, wrote about problems with such courts, including the extension of their jurisdiction. "In this particular the colonists are put under a quite different law from all the rest of the King's subjects: jurisdiction is nowhere else given to courts of admiralty of matters so foreign from their connusance [i.e., cognizance]." A related grievance, although not in the text of the Sugar Act but rather a rule put into effect by administrative procedures, is that "these courts have assumed (I know not by what law) a commission of five per cent to the judge on all seizures condemned. What chance does the subject stand for his right upon the best claim when the judge, condemning, is to have an hundred or perhaps five hundred pounds, and acquitting, less than twenty shillings?"[46]

Section 42 is the apportionment of the seizure of ships and cargo.

XLII. All penalties and forfeitures so recovered . . . be divided, paid, and applied as follows; that is to say, after deducting the charges of prosecution from the gross produce thereof . . . one third part of the net produce shall be paid into the hands of the collector of his Majesty's customs . . . one third part to the governor or commander in chief of the said colony or plantation; and the other third part to the person who shall seize, inform, and sue for the same.

The same section makes an important exception. For "such seizures as shall be made at sea,"

by the commanders or officers of his Majesty's ships or vessels of war duly authorized to make seizures; one moiety [to the king] the other moiety to him or them who shall seize, inform, and sue for the same.

For seizures at sea, one-half of the proceeds would be divided (as decreed in the Hovering Act) among "officers and seamen of such ship or vessel of war who shall make any such seizure." (That is, after a portion is reserved for the admiral of the American fleet.) This section created great controversy and dissention between colonial officials (the collector at each port, and governors) and naval officers. Governor Bernard later (April 28, 1766) wrote the Board of Trade at great length to explain why the apportionment was troublesome. The root problem was that of lack of cooperation. The new policy "has entirely destroyed & rendered impracticable a Connection between the ordinary custom house officers & the Captains of Men of War."[47] In fact, the phrase "made at sea" was so controversial (governors contending the phrase did not include bays and rivers leading to the ocean) that it led to the need for clarification by Parliament in 1765. The clarification is another in 5 George III c. 45, distinctly favoring the navy: "to obviate any doubts that have arisen, or may arise, concerning the construction of the words seizures made at sea," it clarifies that "made at sea" includes, "any where at Sea or in or upon any River, and which shall not be actually made on Shore."[48]

The final five sections, 43-47, are procedures for trials, including those in colonial courts. They often have the effect of protecting customs officers and prosecutors. The effect of these procedures blends with—and exacerbates—the effect of admiralty courts.

XLIII. If the produce of any seizure made in America, shall not be sufficient to answer the expences of condemnation and sale; *or if, upon the trial of any seizure of any ship or goods, a verdict or sentence shall be given for the claimant*, in either of those cases, the charges attending the seizing and prosecuting such ship or goods shall and may, with the consent and approbation of any four of the commissioners of his Majesty's customs, be paid out of any branch of the revenue of customs arising in any of the British colonies or plantations in America.

The situation in which a verdict "shall be given for the claimant" provides a subtle protection for customs officers, dealt with in section 46.

Before the owner had a chance to dispute a seizure, he had to post security sufficient to pay for his own prosecution.

XLIV. No person shall be admitted to enter a claim to any ship or goods seized . . . until sufficient security be first given . . . in the court where such seizure is prosecuted, in the penalty of sixty pounds, to answer the costs and charges of prosecution; and, in default of giving such security, such ship or goods shall be adjudged to be forfeited.

During trial, the burden of proof is on the owner. This is more explicit than a similar provision in the act of 1733.

XLV. [That if] any dispute shall arise whether the customs and duties for such goods have been paid, or [other proof of innocence] the *proof thereof shall lie upon the owner* or claimer of such ship or goods, and *not upon the officer who shall seize or stop the same*.

Section 46 provides protection for a customs officer in the case in which a ship and goods are seized but the shipowner has, in fact, complied with all regulations (that is, an unjustified seizure). One case is that in which the seized ship is released without going before a judge, the other in which the seizure is contested in court and the shipowner prevails. The text starts with the court case.

> XLVI. In case any information shall be commenced [i.e., a formal accusation by the prosecutor] and brought to trial in America [in a court of vice admiralty], on account of any seizure of any ship or goods . . . wherein a verdict or sentence shall be given for the claimer thereof;

That is, the shipowner was innocent and—in the past—might have planned to sue in a common-law court for damages and the cost of the suit. But now,

> [If] it shall appear to the judge . . . that there was a *probable cause of seizure* [then] the defendant [shipowner] shall not be intitled to any costs of suit whatsoever; nor shall the person who seized the said ship or goods, be liable to any action, or other suit or prosecution, on account of such seizure.

The section continues in a similar vein for the situation in which the shipowner is never brought to trial. In such a case, a successful suit by the shipowner can result in his receiving no more than two pence in damages. The defendant in such a suit (the customs official) can be fined no more than one shilling.

The section is long and complex, and full of convoluted statements. Historian Carl Ubbelohde summarizes it this way: "Even if no condemnation was decreed, and the ship and cargo were released from custody and delivered to the owner, the vice-admiralty judge could decide if a probable cause for seizure had existed. If he decided that there had been a probable cause, the judge was authorized to tax the costs of trial on the claimant [shipowner], and no action could be brought against the prosecutor or informer in the common-law courts."[49] In either case, if the judge refused certification of probable cause, section 43 comes into play: four judges (of nine) of the English Customs Board "could authorize reimbursement of the officer for any damages collected from him."[50]

This provision became another American grievance. "Whereas it is good law that all officers seizing goods seize at their peril, and if the goods they seize are not liable to forfeiture they must pay the claimant his cost, and are liable to his action besides . . . both these checks are taken off." In addition, "if the judge of admiralty will certify that there was probable cause of seizure, no action shall be maintained by the claimant though his goods on trial appear to be ever so duly imported and liable to no sort of forfeiture, and he hath been forced to expend ever so much in the defense of them. This last regulation is in the act peculiarly confined to America."[51] There was good rationale (thought the British) for that section and section 47. In the past, customs officers had been sued for damages after the fact (even when performing a legitimate duty). A jury trial in common-law courts in the colonies might result, even in the face of contrary evidence, in a stiff penalty for the customs officer.

Section 47 adds another level of protection for customs officers.

> XLVII. If any action or suit shall be commenced, either in Great Britain or America, against any person or persons *for any thing done in pursuance of this or any other act of parliament relating to his Majesty's customs*, the defendant or defendants [customs officials] in such action or suit may *plead the general issue* and give the said acts, and the special matter, in evidence at any trial to be had thereupon, and that the same was done in pursuance and by the authority of such act; and if it shall appear so to have been done [by the judge], *the jury shall find for the defendant or defendants*.

The final provision provides even more protection than provided in 1733. If the plaintiff, the shipowner, shall

> discontinue his action after the defendant or defendants shall have appeared, or if judgment shall be given upon verdict or demurrer against the plaintiff, the defendant or defendants shall recover treble costs, and have the like remedy for the same as defendants have in other cases by law.

These protections essentially freed customs officers of responsibility for their actions, with some taking advantage of the situation to enrich themselves.

Whately returns to the problem of illicit trade. He explains the dangers. "I do not mean to the Revenue only, but the essential Interest of the Commonweal." British colonies are in danger of becoming colonies of "the Countries they trade to." He forcefully asserts such trade to be substantial. "The Extent of this Commerce, as it is in its Nature private, cannot be certainly known, but that it is now carried to a dangerous Excess, is an indisputable Fact." He explains his basis for claiming widespread smuggling, making a convincing case for wine and tea based on "the Demands of the Colonies upon their Mother Country, being vastly disproportioned to their Consumption." Much of the illicit import of tea is carried not in British or colonial ships, but in shipping of "*the Dutch, the French, the Swedish . . . Companies.*" He ends with a less-convincing argument (merely anecdotal) that the "testimony of all who have ever resided in the Plantations, might be adduced to prove, the great Extent of their illicit Commerce in European Commodities." He alludes again to the "foreign Goods illegally run into the Colonies," and stresses that, "the Suppression of so enormous and dangerous an Evil is a great Object of State, which has been long, far too long neglected: the Laws that have been made for preventing it were sunk into Disuse. . . . That Licentiousness however is now at an End."[52]

Whately is in the British mainstream in believing the Sugar Act was necessary to end the licentiousness. Here is Charles Jenkinson in a letter of January 18, 1765.

The late Law is formed on the principles of the *Act of Navigation*: The intention of it is to *prevent all commerce between our Colonies* and any part of Europe except Great Britain, unless in cases specially allowed, and to permit under certain regulations the commerce of our Continental Colonies with Foreign Islands so as to leave a clear and undoubted proof [?profit] to our own Islands. *With this view all the provisions of it are formed, and as far as it is necessary for this purpose* to restrain the commerce of our Colonies, it is an evil to which *I think they ought to submit for the good of the whole.*[53]

Edmund Burke, however, had a different view (in 1774) about the amount of illicit trade.

> I know, Sir, that great and not unsuccessful pains have been taken to inflame our minds by an outcry, in this House and out of it, that in America *the act of navigation* neither is, or ever was, obeyed. But if you take the Colonies through, I affirm, that its authority never was disputed; that it was no where disputed for any length of time; and *on the whole, that it was well observed.*[54]

After Whately completes discussion of the regulations, he makes a broad summary statement of purpose. "These general Regulations and the particular Provisions of the Act . . . with the zealous Exertion of the civil, the military, and the naval Powers in the Colonies . . . give reasonable Ground to hope that that important Object of Policy, of Commerce, and of Revenue, [namely] the Suppression of the contraband Trade which has prevailed such a length of time in the Colonies, will in a great measure be attained." Whately briefly discusses the amount of revenue likely to be realized from the new regulations but concludes "it is very difficult, if not impossible to form any Calculation," and he "will not even hazard a Conjecture upon it."[55]

It is worth a pause at this point, having just looked at details of the act, to anticipate later objections (1774) of the Americans. Here are the most oppressive provisions. They

- impose duties for the purpose of raising a revenue in America,
- extend the power of the admiralty courts beyond their ancient limits,
- deprive the American subject of trial by jury,
- authorize the judges' certificate [i.e., probable cause] to indemnify the prosecutor from damages, that he might otherwise be liable to,
- [and require] oppressive security from a claimant of ships and goods seized, before he shall be allowed to defend his property.[56]

A RELATED GRIEVANCE: THE CURRENCY ACT

Taxation and regulation were not the only problems facing the Americans in 1764. Hard currency in America was drained off as a result of the unfavorable balance of trade between Great Britain and America; and without local currency, trade suffered for lack of a common medium of exchange. British merchants wanted to restrict the issuance of colonial currency since it led to inflation: good for the debtor Americans, bad for the creditor British merchants.

Following on the heels of the Sugar Act, Parliament passed "An Act to prevent paper bills of credit [in the colonies] from being declared to be a legal tender in payments of money." It became law on April 19, and is often called the *Currency Act* (4 George III c. 34).[57] The act was protested by Americans both before and after its enaction, and was eventually asserted to be a constitutional grievance: it was listed by the First Continental Congress in 1774 as one of the "acts of parliament [that] are infringements and violations of the rights of the colonists."[58]

NEWS TO AMERICA

On May 10, 1764, the first widespread, reliable news of the Sugar Act was published in the *Pennsylvania Gazette* and quickly promulgated throughout the colonies.

> Our other Advices by the Packet are, that a Scheme of Taxation of the American Colonies has for some Time been in Agitation.
>
> That on the Ninth of March, Mr. [Grenville] made a long Harrangue on the melancholy State of the Nation, overloaded with heavy Taxes, and a [heavy] Debt . . . By a Computation, which he laid before the House, £360,000 Sterling per Annum was expended on North America, and therefore it was but reasonable they should support the Troops sent out for their Defence, and all the other particular Expence of the Nation on their Account.

The news was specific about several of the proposed duties, including "a Duty of 3d. per Gallon on foreign Melasses."

> Besides this, an internal Tax was proposed, a Stamp Duty, &c. but many Members warmly opposing it, this was deferred till next

Session; but it was feared that the Tax upon foreign Goods would pass into a Law this Session. That these Colonies are under great Disadvantages in not having sufficient Interest in Parliament; from the Want of which, the West Indies have been able to carry any Point against them.[59]

There was a flood of letters from American agents and friends informing of the Grenville budget speech and giving American leaders insight as to the situation in Parliament. Here is Massachusetts agent Jasper Mauduit writing on April 7.

> The present sense of Parliament is such that I should only flatter and deceive the General Court if I led them to imagine that any one Man of Consequence there would stand up in his place and avow an opinion that America ought not to bear at least the greater part of the expense of its own Government.[60]

BENJAMIN FRANKLIN: INTERNAL AND EXTERNAL TAXES

One aspect of understanding the Sugar Act is appreciation of the American protests (the subject of the next chapter). To understand those protests, it is necessary to understand the distinction made between internal and external taxation—or at least the message conveyed to British leaders regarding *what Americans thought was the distinction*. An important influence on how the British came to their understanding of American thinking was the testimony given by Benjamin Franklin to the House of Commons on February 13, 1766 (in the format of a stylized question-and-answer session). He was famous, the best-known American in London; his statements were taken to be authoritative.

> Q. Did you ever hear the authority of parliament to make laws for America questioned till lately?
> A. The authority of parliament was allowed to be valid in all laws, except such as should lay internal taxes. It was never disputed in *laying duties to regulate commerce.*

This question did not immediately follow the previous, but the juxtaposition is useful.

Q. Was it an opinion in America before 1763, that the parliament had no right to lay taxes and duties there?

A. I had never heard any objection to the right of *laying duties to regulate commerce*; but a right to lay internal taxes was never supposed to be in parliament, as we are not represented there.

In neither answer does he use the phrase "external taxes," referring instead to "laying duties to regulate commerce."

Although Franklin skirted the issue in those answers, he is not always so indirect. Later, he was asked another question on the same topic.

Q. You say the Colonies have always submitted to external taxes, and object to the right of parliament only in laying internal taxes; now can you shew that there is any kind of difference between the two taxes to the Colony on which they may be laid?

He presents his definition of an external tax: a simple statement that might stick in the minds of listeners.

A. I think the difference is very great. *An external tax is a duty laid on commodities imported*; that duty is added to the first cost, and other charges on the commodity, and when it is offered to sale, makes a part of the price. If the people do not like it at that price, they refuse it; they are not obliged to pay it. But an internal tax is forced from the people without their consent, if not laid by their own representatives.

He does not specify the purpose of the duty, whether to regulate commerce or to raise revenue. In either case, it is clear that a "duty laid on commodities imported" is not an internal tax. This establishes the idea that Americans believe a duty collected at an American port—a port duty—is an external tax, and regardless of its purpose is not objectionable.

After Franklin discussed excise taxes, he was asked a similar question.

Q. You say [Americans] do not object to the right of parliament in laying duties on goods to be paid on their importation; now, is there any kind of difference between a duty on the importation of goods and an excise on their consumption?

The question prompts further approval of external taxation.

A. Yes; a very material one; an excise, for the reasons I just mentioned, they think you can have no right to lay within their country. *But the sea is yours*; you maintain, by your fleets, the safety of navigation in it, and keep it clear of pirates; *you may have therefore a natural and equitable right to some toll or duty* on merchandizes carried through that part of your dominions, towards defraying the expence you are at in ships to maintain the safety of that carriage.

In answer to several questions referring to the Pennsylvania assembly, Franklin makes a comment generally applicable to the definition of taxes (not necessarily adding clarity to the discussion). "By taxes they mean internal taxes; by duties they mean customs; these are their ideas of the language." (An alternate source quotes Franklin slightly differently, using the phrase *external taxes*. "By the word taxes they have always considered internal taxes only, and when they mean external taxes, they use the word duties.")[61]

A related question challenges him to justify the right to be taxed only with consent or the consent of elected representatives (and not taxed by Parliament). He invokes, "*the common rights of Englishmen*, as declared by Magna Charta, and the Petition of Right." That answer brings forth a question that could be difficult to handle.

Q. Then may they not, by the same interpretation object to the parliament's right of *external* taxation?

He makes this clever answer, avoiding the question, but making a provocative point.

A. They never have hitherto. Many arguments have been lately used here to shew them that there is no difference, and that *if you have no right to tax them internally, you have none to tax them externally*, or make any other law to bind them. At present they do not reason so, but in time they may possibly be convinced by these arguments.

That amusing response garnered chuckles, but no serious follow-up question.[62]

Use of the phrase "external tax" was exceedingly troublesome, despite Franklin's straightforward statement that "an external tax is a duty laid on commodities imported." The confusing aspect of the vocabulary is that there were two sorts of duties laid on imported goods: those for the regulation of trade, and those for the purpose of raising revenue. Franklin, of course, has no problem; any duty is an external tax.

The American distinction between internal and external taxes was short-lived, ending two years later. During its lifetime, however, the distinction (whether or not there was a true difference) influenced the course of events of the Revolution. According to Bernard Bailyn, "By 1765 English opponents of American claims were imputing to the distinction between 'internal' and 'external' taxation . . . an importance and a rigor that had never been intended for it, and that made it vulnerable to attacks no one had expected it to have to withstand."[63]

EDMUND BURKE: COLONIAL POLICY AND THE SUGAR ACT

Edmund Burke made his now-famous *Speech on American Taxation* in the House of Commons on April 19, 1774, on the occasion of a debate to repeal the tax on tea. He scolds the House for its change in colonial policy in 1764, the "grand manoeuvre" being passage of the Sugar Act.

Whether you were right or wrong in establishing the Colonies on the principles of commercial monopoly, rather than on that of revenue, is at this day a problem of mere speculation. *You cannot have both by the same authority.* To join together the restraints of an universal internal and external monopoly, with an universal internal and external taxation, is an unnatural union; perfect uncompensated slavery.

He pinpoints the Sugar Act as marking the beginning of a new policy.

The grand manoeuvre in that business of new regulating the colonies, was the 15th act of the fourth of George 3; which . . . opened *a new principle: and here properly began the second period of the policy of this country with regard to the colonies*; by which the scheme of a regular plantation parliamentary revenue was adopted in theory, and settled in practice. A revenue not substituted in the place of, but superadded to, a monopoly; which monopoly was enforced at the same time with additional strictness, and the execution put into military hands.

The act was full of assertions of taxation.

This act, Sir, had for the first time the title of "granting duties in the colonies and plantations of America;" and for the first time it was asserted in the preamble, "that it was just and necessary that a revenue should be raised there." Then came the technical words of "giving and granting;" and thus a complete American Revenue Act was made in all the forms, and with a full avowal of the right, equity, policy, and even necessity of taxing the colonies, without any formal consent of theirs.

He points out good reason for the Americans to be concerned about the future. The colonies had long accepted that duties were paid on goods being transshipped through England, but this is the first distinct colonial tax, with duties being collected at American ports. He then points out phrases that are of considerable importance to understanding the events of the years following 1764.

There are contained also in the preamble to that Act these very remarkable words—the Commons, &c.—"being desirous to make some provision in the present session of Parliament towards raising the said revenue." *By these words it appeared to the colonies that this act was but a beginning of sorrows*; that every session was to produce something of the same kind; that we were to go on from day to day, in charging them with such taxes as we pleased, for such a military force as we should think proper. Had this plan been pursued, it was evident that the Provincial Assemblies, in which the Americans felt all their portion of importance, and beheld their sole image of freedom, were *ipso facto* annihilated.[64]

The Americans did not have any rights they could rely upon to prevent the charging of "such taxes as we pleased" by Parliament. This, in turn, led to American apprehension about future British actions. If the Americans seem to have overreacted to a relatively minor burden (an attitude common in Britain) it was often a reaction not to what Parliament had done but to what might be done in the future.

Bernard Bailyn has made the point that the Sugar Act of 1764 "was the first unmistakable proof to the colonists that the Grenville administration had seriously undertaken the revision of existing relationships between England and America."[65] Its most important feature, the greatest American grievance, is that it was an act of revenue. No doubt about it. However foggy the terrain in 1764, later events proved it to be a tax. The key distinction between the Sugar Act of 1764 and all previous acts that imposed duties on imports is that it was genuinely enacted for—and stated as having the purpose of—raising revenue. It was this parliamentary taxation that began the empire-shaking dispute between Britain and the American colonies.

Five

Protest

"All Impositions, *whether they be internal Taxes or Duties paid* for what we consume, equally diminish the Estates upon which they are charged."

—New York, 1764

"Subjects in the Colonies . . . *may be subjected therein to such Duties*, Charges and Regulations as the supreme Power may judge proper to establish."

—Connecticut, 1764

A MERICAN PROTESTS AGAINST THE SUGAR ACT OF 1764 EMPHASIZED the economic burden of duties placed on sugar, rum, and molasses of foreign colonies. The most strident protests were against what was perceived as a prohibitive duty on molasses ("being so much higher than it can possibly bear"). Further protest dealt with the expanded jurisdiction of admiralty courts and new regulations that placed undue burdens on trade. Although there were some ripples of protest against the taxation of the Sugar Act, they were lost in the tsunami of protest against unconstitutional stamp duties, both in 1764 and 1765. There was good reason for such mild American protest. As historian Gordon Wood put it, "Since they had accepted the Navigation Acts in the seventeenth century, they had not generally denied Parliament's authority to regulate their trade, which was what the Sugar Act seemed to be. Consequently, their constitutional protests against it were few and far between."[1]

It is important to examine the American protests as they highlight those aspects of the British change in colonial policy that were most objectionable and were most consequential to the American Revolution. An equally important reason for this examination is to understand the message received by British leaders: that internal taxation was unacceptable to Americans as a violation of their rights, while customs duties were acceptable external taxes within the authority of Parliament.[2]

THE PROTESTS OF 1764

The protests of late 1764—in contrast to the reasons against renewal voiced early in the year—dealt not only with the recent Sugar Act, but also with the threat of stamp duties. The protest to the planned taxation was universal, that such stamp duties would be unconstitutional, violating the rights of the colonists in disregard for the *rights of Englishmen*. However, in almost all formal positions taken by the colonies, the Sugar Act was seen as trade regulation. The act of 1764 seemed to be a continuation of the act of 1733, including duties being given and granted to the king. An added statement of purpose that new regulations should be established for "improving the revenue" was followed by the additional reason of "extending and securing the navigation and commerce." Even "necessary that a revenue be raised" did not ring alarm bells.[3]

New York

New York was the exception. It was the only colony to submit a petition asserting that duties for revenue were a constitutional grievance. The petition to the House of Commons was approved on October 18.

> Since all Impositions, *whether they be internal Taxes or Duties paid* for what we consume, equally diminish the Estates upon which they are charged; what avails it to any People, by which of them they are impoverished? Every Thing will be given up to preserve Life; and though there is a Diversity in the Means, yet, the

whole Wealth of a Country may be as effectually drawn off by the Exaction of Duties, *as by any other Tax* upon their Estates.

New York insists that Parliament should

charge our Commerce with no other Duties than a necessary Regard to the particular Trade of Great Britain evidently demands; but leave it to the legislative Power of the Colony to impose all other Burthens upon it's own People, which the publick Exigences may require.[4]

New York not only calls out the duties as being equivalent to "any other Tax," the petition also points out the irregular nature of duties other than those demanded by the "particular Trade of Great Britain." This line of thinking ends with a bit of wry understatement. "Latterly, the Laws of Trade seem to have been framed without an Attention to this fundamental Claim." Such interference with colonial commerce infringes on colonial rights in the sense of being unjust, an abuse of parliamentary power.

Connecticut

The stance of Connecticut was established by an essay prepared by Governor Thomas Fitch; it was published as a pamphlet, largely written in the summer and approved by the assembly in October: *Reasons why the British Colonies in America should not be charged with Internal Taxes*. The essay denies Parliament the right to tax the colonies; but of greater importance is what it concedes; Fitch makes the specific assertion that duties for revenue are within the authority of Parliament. Since "the Colonies are so many Governments independent [of] each other . . . they can only establish Regulations within and for themselves respectively." Therefore, regarding trade, "Propriety, Conveniency and even Necessity require that they should be subject to some General Superintendency and Controul," such control belonging to Parliament as the "supreme Director over all His Majesty's Dominions."

It is humbly conceived, that the Subjects in the Colonies may enjoy their Rights, Privileges and Properties, as Englishmen, and yet, for political Reasons, be restrained from some particular Correspondence or Branches of Trade and Commerce, or may be subjected therein to such Duties, Charges and Regulations as the supreme Power *may judge proper to establish* as so many Conditions of enjoying such Trade. Reasons of State may render it expedient to prohibit some Branches of Trade and to burden others.

Fitch even suggests specific duties for revenue: "a Duty (if thought necessary and proper) on the Importation of Negroes, and on the Fur Trade, &c." (It is no surprise that the duties he suggests would have no adverse effect on Connecticut.) There is no ambiguity here: the duties he suggests are *intended to raise revenue*. At the end of the essay, Fitch is explicit in his request that Parliament "have a tender regard for the rights and immunities of the King's subjects in the American colonies and *charge no internal taxations upon them without their consent.*"[5]

Fitch was not alone in his approval of duties for the sake of raising revenue, or of his suggesting specific goods to be taxed. For example, in February 1764, Benjamin Franklin had written Pennsylvania agent Richard Jackson that, "If Money must be raised from us to support 14 Batallions, as you mention, I think . . . a moderate Duty on Foreign Mellasses may be collected; when a high one could not. The same on foreign Wines; and a Duty not only on Tea, but on all East India Goods might perhaps not be amiss, as they are generally rather Luxuries than Necessaries."[6]

Massachusetts

The Massachusetts stance was muddled, different positions being taken by radical patriots in the assembly and the conservative members of the council. The eventual official position of the colony offered no constitutional grievance against the duties of the Sugar Act; but before that position was formally expressed, earlier statements objecting to Sugar Act duties as taxation became well known.

On May 24, at a Boston town meeting, a committee led by patriot firebrand Samuel Adams prepared instructions to the Boston delegates in the House of Representatives (including James Otis, Oxenbridge Thacher, and Thomas Cushing). The instructions are critical of the delay in dealing with "the intention of the ministry to burden us with new taxes." They stress, "There is now no room for further delay; we therefore expect that you will use your earliest endeavours in the General Assembly that such methods may be taken as will effectually prevent these proceedings against us."

> What still heightens our apprehensions is that these unexpected proceedings *may be preparatory to new taxations upon us; for if our trade may be taxed, why not our lands?* Why not the produce of our lands and everything we possess or make use of? This we apprehend annihilates our charter right to govern and tax ourselves. It strikes at our British privileges, which, as we have never forfeited them, we hold in common with our fellow subjects who are natives of Britain. If taxes are laid upon us in any shape without our having a legal representation where they are laid, are we not reduced from the character of free subjects to the miserable state of tributary slaves?

And at the end:

> As his Majesty's other northern American colonies are embark'd with us in this most important bottom, we further desire you to use your endeavors, that their weight may be added to that of this province: that by *the united application of all who are aggrieved,* All may happily obtain redress.[7]

On June 13, the House of Representatives sent instructions to agent Jasper Mauduit. (The assembly, acting irregularly, prepared and sent the letter without seeking concurrence from the council.) Referring to both the Sugar Act and the impending stamp duties, the assembly denied any "Right in the Parliament of Great-Britain to impose Duties and Taxes upon a People who are not represented in the House of Commons," and directed Mauduit "to remonstrate against these measures, and if possible, to obtain a repeal of the Sugar Act, and prevent the imposition of any *further Duties or Taxes* on these Colonies."[8] The letter was a significant milestone in the development of colonial protest. Thomas Hutchinson, more than a decade later (residing in London, no longer a British official in Massachusetts), as part of his refutation of the American Declaration of Independence, asserted that "the Colony of Massachuset's Bay was more affected by the Act for granting duties, than any other Colony. More molasses, the principal article from which any duty could arise, was distilled into spirits in that Colony than in all the rest. The Assembly of Massachuset's Bay, therefore, was the first that took any publick notice of the [Sugar Act], and the *first which ever took exception* to the right of Parliament to impose Duties or Taxes on the Colonies. This they did in a letter to their Agent in the summer of 1764."[9]

On June 25, the assembly wrote the other colonies. The letter dealt with, "the late Act of Parliament relating to the Sugar Trade with Foreign Colonies, and the Resolutions of the House of Commons relating to Stamp Duties and other Taxes proposed to be laid on the British colonies." The letter suggested united action, that the assembly was "desirous of the united Assistance of the several Colonies in a Petition."[10]

On June 29, Governor Bernard sent the Board of Trade copies of the June 13 and June 25 letters. He added these comments on the letter to other governments. He perceives that the letter is intended

> to lay a foundation for connecting the demagogues of the several Governments in America to join together in opposition to all orders from Great Britain which don't square with their notions of the rights of the people. Perhaps I may be too suspicious; a little time will show whether I am or not.[11]

Continuing their agitation, the assembly prepared a bold protest to recent actions as a proposed address to the king and both houses of Parliament. It included the following phrase, referring to both the duties of the Sugar Act and the threatened stamp duties: "*that we look upon those duties as a tax*."[12] That draft address, sent to the council for concurrence on October 22, was rejected.

The resulting compromise petition—the formal position of Massachusetts—was approved on November 3, and addressed to the House of Commons only; it expressed a grievance about the duties of the Sugar Act as an economic burden, raising no issue that the duties were beyond the legitimate authority of Parliament. The "Duties laid upon foreign sugars & molasses" both in 1733 and 1764, must have "the effect of an absolute prohibition." If not repealed, the duties "will lessen the consumption of the manufactures of Great Britain." The petition even makes only a modest protest to the planned stamp duties. After a statement of hardships,

> Your Petitioners, therefore, most humbly pray that they may be relieved from the burdens which they have humbly represented to have been brought upon them by the late Act of Parliament [and] that the privileges of the Colonies *relative to their internal taxes* which they have so long enjoyed may still be continued to them.[13]

Other Colonies

As the newly elected speaker of the Pennsylvania assembly, Benjamin Franklin sent agent Richard Jackson instructions on September 22, dealing with "Stamp Duties, and other Taxes, proposed to be laid on the British Colonies." The instructions are focused on proposed duties, pointing out that such measures would be inconsistent "with the Rights and Privileges . . . granted and confirmed to the People of this Colony." They admonish him to prevail "on the Parliament to lay aside their Intention of imposing Stamp Duties, *or laying any other Impositions or Taxes whatsoever on the Colonies*, which may be destructive of their respective Rights." Regarding the existing situation, "Exert your Endeavours to obtain a Repeal, or at least an Amendment, of the Act for regulating the Sugar Trade, which we apprehend *must prove extremely detrimental to the Trade* of the Continental Colonies in America."[14]

Rhode Island petitioned the king on November 29. "The restraints and burdens laid on the trade of these colonies by a late act of Parliament are such, as if continued, must ruin it. The commerce of this colony dependeth ultimately on foreign molasses, and the duty on that being so much higher than it can possibly bear, must prevent its importation."

The petition goes on to state the grievance about denial of trial by jury.

> The extensive powers given by the [Sugar Act] to the courts of

vice admiralty in America, have a tendency, in a great measure, to deprive the colonies of *that darling privilege, trials by juries, the unalienable birthright of every Englishman;* . . . and herein we are unhappily distinguished from our fellow subjects in Britain.[15]

The situation was the same throughout the colonies; while aggressively rejecting the planned taxation by stamp duties, and including a grievance about deprivation of the right of trial by jury, American protests complained only that the Sugar Act "must prove extremely detrimental" to their trade. The protests largely ignored the constitutional aspects of Sugar Act duties, instead replaying the reasons against renewal expressed by the northern colonies in early 1764.[16]

Individual Objections

In the summer, Thomas Whately wrote two correspondents in America. The responses give additional insight into the nature of the Sugar Act.

Whately wrote his Connecticut friend Jared Ingersoll (an important lawyer, influential politician, and later London agent for the colony). Ingersoll received the (undated) letter on July 4, responding on July 6. He wrote, "that the foreign Molasses will bear a Duty of One penny half penny at most." Since it will be impossible to stop smuggling at the level of three pence, "I verily believe there won't be Enough Collected in ye Course of ten years to Defray ye expence of fitting out one the least frigate for an American Voyage, & that the *whole Labour will be like burning a Barn to roast an Egg.*"

> Was the Duty lowered to where I have mentioned, the Merchants would pay it without any men of war to Compel him to it—he would pay it rather than run the risque of ye Custom house officer alone & partly by reason of his having been used to pay a Sum not much short of that [as the cost of smuggling]. Perhaps 'tis the Intention of Parliament that *the Duty should amount to a prohibition of ye trade*—why they should Aim at that indeed I cannot conceive with the Ideas I now have of things.[17]

On June 8, Whately wrote John Temple. Temple's response is of particular significance since he was an important British official in

America. As surveyor general of customs for the five northern colonies, he supervised the customs collectors at each port. He responded on September 10.

> Molosses is the principal article on [which] any money worth mentioning can be raised, & on that I fear Parliament will find they have left too large a duty in 3d a gallon. The trade will either decline or methods will be found out thro corrupt officers in the West Indies to naturalize foreign produce there, & introduce it to the northern Colonies as Brittish growth.

He introduces a creative idea: a duty of only two pence, but "on the produce of Brittish as well as foreign molasses; ... Our own sugar planters could have no reasonable objection to the duty's being general, for the molosses they export is so very inconsiderable that 'tis not worth mentioning."

> With them 'tis all turned into rum, & principally sent to Great Brittain. Had the duty extended to molosses of what produce soever there would have been no possible means of its escaping the duty, & 2d a gallon, I believe, is full as much as the trade can bear & continue to flourish.[18]

Influence of the Impending Stamp Act

An essay of early 1768 explained why the Americans at first (1764) protested only the economic burden of the Sugar Act.

> If anyone should observe that no opposition has been made to the legality of the 4th Geo. III. Chap. 15, which is the first act of parliament that ever imposed duties on the importations in America *for the expressed purpose of raising a revenue there*; I answer—

The Sugar Act text is ambiguous.

> That tho' the act expressly mentions the raising of a revenue in America, yet it seems that it had as much in view the "improving and securing the trade between the same and Great Britain," which words are part of its title.

The threat of the Stamp Act affected protests to the Sugar Act. Since it was doubtful "whether the intention of the 4th Geo. III. Chap. 15" was to regulate trade, or to raise a revenue, "the minds of the people here were wholly engrossed by the *terror of the Stamp Act*, then impending over them, about the intention of which there could be no doubt."[19]

Much later in the controversy (1775), as explanation for British actions in 1765, a pamphlet prepared on behalf of the ministry put forth the British viewpoint regarding the American stance on duties and taxation. It asserted that although the Americans in 1764 remonstrated

> against some of the provisions of [the Sugar Act], they at that time did not so much as argue against the principle. They conceived, and endeavoured to shew, that the power of parliament had been impoliticly exercised; but they did not yet go so far as to say, that the power itself was unconstitutional.

Even further, "It is only from the time of the Americans receiving account of the passing of the Stamp Act that [appeared] the great discontents that arose among them." And any contention "that the power itself was unconstitutional" did not arise from the Sugar Act, but rather as part of "the disturbances caused by the Stamp Act."[20]

1765: TAXATION AND RESISTANCE

Parliament made no move to conciliate the Americans—even refusing to accept American petitions of 1764—and in early 1765 passed the Stamp Act despite the constitutionally based arguments of the Americans.

During this period of consideration of the bill for stamp duties, Grenville—with full knowledge of the American grievance—had no intention of reducing the duties of the Sugar Act; he did not even wish to hear of any problems. On January 12, Joseph Harrison wrote Surveyor-General John Temple about his interaction with Grenville. "I found that he did not like to hear that there should be any surmise of [the Sugar Act] not being likely to produce the sum expected, which I am affraid has been estimated much too high, and I am very sensible will fall vastly short of the sanguine hopes that have been entertained about it."[21] (Harrison is a person of some significance. Earlier collector of customs at the port of New Haven, in 1765 he was a secretary to Lord Rockingham, and was later collector of customs for Boston.)

On February 6, the committee of the whole house was instructed "to consider further of Ways and Means for raising a Revenue . . ."[22] Despite some lively opposition to its passage, the question was never in doubt, many members having been offended by the "high tones" of the colonial protests against internal taxation. Grenville dismissed the American objections to the planned stamp duties by pointing out a critical characteristic that was impossible for Parliament to accept.

> The objection of the colonies is from the general right of mankind not to be taxed but by their representatives. *This goes to all laws in general.*

William Beckford made a comment that reinforced the British understanding of the American position. He supported the right "of taxing the imports and exports of the colonies" and—the most important point for us to hear—that "the colonies all admit this principle." But he warned his colleagues that such acceptance would not extend to stamp duties. "The North Americans do not think an internal and external duty the same."[23]

Whately, writing Temple a few days later, explains the position of the House of Commons. He calls the bill a "great measure,"

> on account of the important point it establishes, the right of Parliament to lay an internal tax upon the Colonies. We wonder here that it ever was doubted. There is not a single member of Parliament to be found that will dispute it, & the proposition of a stamp duty seem'd so reasonable when made last week to the House, that but 49 divided against it, when 245 were for it, & the expediency only was debated. This puts an end to all opposition to the principle of the bill, & now the rates are the only question.[24]

On February 11, Jared Ingersoll (then in London) wrote Connecticut Governor Fitch. He reported Grenville's introduction of the bill for stamp duties, during which he denied "any Distinction between what is called an internal & external Tax as to the point of the Authority imposing such taxes."[25]

After passage of the Stamp Act, the story of the year 1765 is dominated by American protests and violent resistance.[26] Colonial petitions and resolves offer little additional insight into the Sugar Act. Although the objection to taxation was universal, objections to the Sugar Act continued to be largely based on the adverse effect of regulation of trade.

The Stamp Act Congress in October, in what can be taken as the best and final consensus opinion of the colonies in 1765, made a forthright case against any taxation by Parliament, but never stated that duties of the Sugar Act constituted taxation. The congress did object to admiralty courts and trade restrictions, and asked for repeal of the Stamp Act and "other acts," even the several acts "imposing duties and taxes on the colonies;" but the condemnation was never specific, never naming the Sugar Act as a statute to be repealed. [27]

RIGHT TO IMPOSE EXTERNAL TAXES?

Prominent American loyalist Daniel Leonard criticized the American taxation attitude in an open letter published in the *Massachusetts Gazette* on January 16, 1775.

> It is curious indeed to trace the denial and oppugnation to the supreme authority of the state. When the stamp-act was made, the authority of parliament to impose internal taxes was denied *but their right to impose external ones*, or in other words, to lay duties upon goods and merchandize *was admitted*.[28]

Then he went on to accuse the colonies of shifting their ground, that they later denied the right of Parliament to levy duties for revenue.

John Adams expressed the contrary American view, published in the *Boston Gazette* on March 13. Adams quoted the statement by Leonard (regarding "the authority of parliament"), then asserted that, "This is a total misapprehension of the declared opinions of people at those times. The authority of parliament to lay taxes for a revenue has been always generally denied."[29]

Edmund Burke addressed the nature of the American protests. "When the first American Revenue Act (the Act in 1764, imposing the port duties) passed, the Americans did not object to the principle. It is true they touched it but very tenderly. . . . The duties were port duties, *like those they had been accustomed to bear.*"[30] As a consequence, British officials believed the duties of the Sugar Act were acceptable to Americans, never hearing any consistent message that the duties were objectionable as a violation of colonial rights. In fact, the British later justified their understanding of the American position by using phrases such as: "those very duties which . . . we were told they were so willing to pay," and that we were "misled by the Americans themselves."

Although American legislative protests were largely ignored, violence and threats of violence against the stamp distributors—essentially nullifying the Stamp Act—led to British repeal of the act, and to reconsideration of the new commercial policies.

Six

The British Retreat

"You will have the Molasses duty reduced to 1d & a new Regulation of the Admiralty Courts; a Bill being soon to be brought into the House for that purpose & some other advantages to Trade which will be supported by the Body of Merchants."
—An American agent, March 17, 1766

"A Revision of the late American Trade Laws is going to be the immediate Object of Parliament. [This will] give to the Trade and Interests of America every relief which the true State of their circumstances demands."
—Secretary of State Conway, March 31, 1766

I N 1766, IN RESPONSE TO AMERICAN RESISTANCE TO TAXATION OF the Stamp Act, the British retreated from the aggressive colonial policy formulated in 1763. The most important feature of the retreat was the repeal of the Stamp Act.[1] Notification to America of the repeal included a promise to resolve grievances regarding the need for commercial reform. Ominously, however, the repeal was accompanied by a declaration of Parliament's full authority over colonial affairs.

This chapter describes the attitude of British leaders, and information flowing to America regarding progress toward repeal and commercial reform. Development and passage of the once-again-revised Sugar Act—the most meaningful commercial reform resulting from American protests—is addressed in the following chapter.

END OF A MINISTRY

In mid-1765, as a result of internal British politics, the king replaced George Grenville and his ministry with a new administration headed by the young (age thirty-five) and inexperienced Marquis of Rockingham. On July 10, 1765, King George III summoned Grenville. As he lay down his office, Grenville predicted that the plan of the new ministry would be the

> total subversion of every act of [Grenville's]; that nothing having been undertaken as a measure without His Majesty's approbation, he knew not how he would let himself be persuaded to see it in so different a light, and most particularly on the regulations concerning the Colonies.

Grenville announced his intent to argue for a continuation of the policies he had instituted. He further advised the king that as he

> valued his own safety, not to suffer any one to advise him to separate or draw the line between his British and American dominions; that his Colonies were the richest jewel of his Crown [and] that if any man ventured to defeat the regulations laid down for the Colonies by a slackness in the execution, [the king] should look upon him as a criminal and the betrayer of his country.[2]

Had Grenville remained at the head of government, he would have demanded enforcement of the Stamp Act—no British retreat, perhaps leading to armed conflict with America, civil war in 1766 rather than a decade later. Rockingham had no such strong opinions. In fact, he was perceived as being indecisive, and as forming a weak ministry. "Few Administrations could have begun less auspiciously, at least in the view of contemporaries. Charles Townshend's celebrated epithet—'a Lutestring ministry; fit only for the summer'—with its implication that the Ministers were incapable of facing a Parliamentary session in the winter, was wholly representative of current opinion."[3]

SUPPORT FOR COMMERCIAL REFORM

By late 1765, Rockingham realized that American resistance to the Stamp Act was a serious threat to the stability of the empire. He took considerable care to look into alternatives, whether to enforce the act, to revise it, or to repeal it. His efforts were directed (despite some early vacillation) toward repeal. He also understood that both American and British merchants believed that revision of the duties and regulations of the Sugar Act was a necessary condition to return trade to a harmonious and profitable status. Nonetheless, the first step had to be repeal.

An integral part of the repeal effort by Rockingham was the quelling of parliamentary concerns that repeal would be an admission of weakness. He worked to reassure members of Parliament that the Americans would be thankful and appreciative. Merchants' testimony in the House of Commons in early 1766 established a foundation. "If the Stamp Act was repealed the House would soon have specimens of that gratitude."[4] Such testimony was important because opponents of repeal, the opposition led by Grenville, predicted that Americans would take the position that Parliament had given up authority to levy taxes, even that the Navigation Acts had no force. In addition to calming Parliament, Rockingham needed to ensure that the Americans did not crow and strut, gloating over repeal as a success for their violent resistance. It was necessary that he would, after a repeal, be proven correct in his prediction that the Americans would not view the repeal as representing a victory over a weak British government.

Rockingham lacked strong support in Parliament; as a consequence, seeking allies, he formed a close alliance with British merchants. Having no strong opinion on policy, he was greatly influenced by the attitudes of those merchants. His closest collaboration was with Barlow Trecothick (a wealthy and politically active London merchant and later a member of the House of Commons), who by December 4 organized and became chairman of a committee of North American merchants. (The phrase "American merchants" in this context means the British merchants whose principal trade was with the colonies.) The committee of merchants was formed in

London for the purpose of agitating for reform of policy toward America. British merchants had long been advocates of easing restrictions on American trade (and hence counter to interests of the British sugar islands) and were focused on ensuring that, after the expected repeal of the Stamp Act, nothing was to interfere with commercial reform.[5] In a general meeting of merchants, the committee was given this charge:

> to consider the best Method of Application for Procuring *the Relief and Encouragement of the North American trade*, and to apply to the Outports and to the Manufacturing Citys and Towns for their Concurrence and Assistance.[6]

On December 6, the committee sent a letter (drafted by Trecothick in cooperation with Rockingham) to the port and manufacturing towns. We ask your "Concurrence and Assistance in *support of a regular Application to Parliament*, or otherwise [by] a Petition from your Body."
They define the style of the desired petition.

> We desire to unite with you in a Measure so essential to the *best Interests of Great Britain*, wishing to have your Sentiments on the Subject, thro' the Course of which, we mean to take for our Guide the Interest of these Kingdoms, it being our Opinion that conclusive Arguments for granting every Ease or Advantage the North Americans can with Propriety desire may be fairly deduced from that principle only.[7]

The subtext is that the requested petitions avoid the subject of American resistance.
On December 14, 1765, newly appointed Massachusetts agent Dennys De Berdt (a wealthy and politically active London-based merchant) wrote Samuel White, speaker of the assembly.

> I have the pleasure to acquaint you the ministry are intirely convinced of the Bad Tendency of the late regulations & disposed to relieve you, but expect a warm opposition from the old ministry [i.e., Grenville] & what they Call the Country Party; you may de-

pend nothing in my power shall be wanting to serve you as I am fully persuaded the Interest of the Colonies & their Mother Country are Inseperable & with their affection mutual.

I have further the satisfaction to Inform you that the merchants of London are warmly espous[ing] your Cause, [and] have chosen a Committee to Carry on an application to parliament. [The committee has] sent Circular Letters to the Principal Cities & Towns throughout the Kingdom to Join their Weight and influence with ours & then to Bring Both City & Country [as] well as your own Petittions in aid to the ministry which I hope will be a way superior to any party opposition that can be made against us.[8]

Trecothick's efforts in December resulted in a January 1766 flood of petitions supporting repeal from the port and manufacturing towns. The petition from London, read in the House of Commons on January 17, included these key points regarding the importance of commerce with America:

That the petitioners have been long concerned in carrying on the trade between this country and the British colonies on the continent of North America; and that they have annually exported very large quantities of British manufactures [a long list of products] by all which many thousand manufacturers, seamen and labourers, have been employed, to the very great and increasing benefit of this nation.

In return for these exports, the petitioners have received from the colonies [many raw materials], bills of exchange and bullion, obtained by the colonists in payment for articles of their produce not required for the British market [i.e., the horses, lumber, and provisions, an issue ever since 1733], and therefore exported to other places.

The petition emphasizes that the trade is vital to "the Commercial System of this Nation" and must not suffer any interference.[9]

Rockingham, having staked the reputation of his administration on American quiet acceptance of the repeal of the Stamp Act, worked closely with the London merchants to condition Americans to not revel in victory over Parliament. Rockingham's strategy is revealed by this letter of February 12, 1766, from the Earl of Dartmouth, enclosing an essay (the author being Sir George Savile, at that time no friend of America) called, "Considerations on the Repeal of the Stamp [Act], and recommending a suitable behaviour to the Americans on that occasion." The essay goes on at length advocating the American response be that of "submission and gratitude." Dartmouth ends a lengthy quote of the Savile essay with, "This is the idea which I think *might be instilled and cultivated in the colonies by merchants to their correspondents*; and I think, in our present situation, a very great deal depends on its being done universally and immediately."[10] The London committee of North American merchants wrote letters to their correspondents in the colonies. Following the guidance of the Savile essay, the letters were intended to mold the American response into expressions of gratitude for the munificence of Parliament.

NEWS TO AMERICA

An early indication of commercial reform is shown by this letter to Lieutenant Governor Hutchinson from his friend William Bollan (previously the agent for Massachusetts) on October 14, 1765, regarding a conversation with the prime minister.

> The Marquis said that His Majesty and his present ministers were inclined to relieve the American trade in general in all points *wherein it was improperly curbed* and put the whole upon the best foot for the common good of the Kingdom and the colonies.[11]

Early in 1766, the likelihood of commercial reform became even clearer. Here is a letter from a British merchant in Bristol, Henry Cruger, Jr., writing his father in New York on February 14. (Cruger was politically active, educated in America, and later a representative to the Commons from Bristol.) He describes goings-on in Parliament, including that "All the principal Manufacturing Towns have sent Petitions for a Repeal of the Stamp Act." He ends on an optimistic note.

> The Parliament have not yet done any thing about the Sugar Act and other destructive restraints on your trade; it will come as soon

as ever the Stamp Act is settled. I imagine they will rescind all the restrictive clauses, and *grant you everything you ask.* Their Eyes are at last open'd and they seem convinc'd what vast Benefit will accrue to this Kingdom by giving you almost an unlimitted trade, so farr as doth not interfere with British Manufactures. The West Indians are collecting all their Force to oppose us; I have reason to say they will at length be defeated. . . . *The Duty on Melasses will be reduced to 1d per Gallon.*[12]

In the House of Commons, following a decisive vote that made repeal of the Stamp Act all but a formality, the chair of the American Committee (a committee of the whole house) reported on February 21 that "he was directed by the Committee to move, that they may have Leave to sit again."[13] The importance of this for the Sugar Act is that it was an indicator that commercial reform would be seriously addressed. (The chair of the committee was wealthy merchant Rose Fuller, a major landowner in the West Indies, principal spokesman for Jamaica, and a prominent member of the West Indian Committee.)

Benjamin Franklin wrote two letters on February 27. The first was to Charles Thomson (a patriot leader in Philadelphia).

We at length, after a long and hard Struggle, have gain'd so much Ground, that there is now little Doubt the Stamp Act will be repealed, and reasonable Relief given us besides in our Commercial Grievances.

Americans must support their friends in Parliament.

I trust the Behaviour of the Americans on the Occasion, will be *so prudent, decent, and grateful, as that their Friends here will have no reason to be ashamed*; and that our Enemies, who predict that the Indulgence of Parliament will only make us more insolent and ungovernable, may find themselves, and be found, false Prophets.

The second, to Hugh Roberts (a Philadelphia merchant and close friend to Franklin), conveys the same sentiment.

We have been often between Hope and Despair; but now the Day begins to clear, the Ministry are fix'd for us, and we have obtain'd a Majority in the House of Commons for Repealing the Stamp Act, *and giving us Ease in every Commercial Grievance.* God grant that no bad News of further Excesses in America may arrive to strengthen our Adversaries and weaken the Hands of our Friends, before this good Work is quite compleated.

The Partizans of the late Ministry have been strongly crying out Rebellion, and calling for Force to be sent against America! The Consequence might have been terrible! but milder Measures have prevailed. I hope, nay I am confident, America will Show itself grateful to Britain on this Occasion, and behave prudently and decently.[14]

On February 28, the London committee of North American merchants wrote their American counterparts to advocate proper conduct. The merchants based the text of this letter on the Savile essay submitted to Rockingham by Dartmouth on February 12; much is verbatim.

It had been a constant Argument against the Repeal, that in case it should take place . . . the Colonies will understand very well, *that what is pretended to be adopted,* on mere Commercial Principle of Expedience, *is really yielded* thro' fear; and amounts to a tacit but effectual Surrender of its right or at least a tacit Compact that it will never use it.

Therefore, it is important that the Americans should accept the pretense of repeal as being based on commercial principles, and not a retreat on principle or as yielding to American resistance.

The Event will justify those Arguments in the strongest manner, if the Colonies should triumph on the Repeal, and affect to seize the yielding of Parliament, as a point gain'd over Parliamentary Authority. The Opposition (from whom the Colonies have suffered so much) would then throw in the Teeth of our Friends see your Work—it is as we said—it is but too well prov'd what use the Colonies make of your Weak and timid Measures.

On the Contrary, if Duty, Submission, and Gratitude, be the returns made by the Colonies, then, our Friends may exult, they may say, we are in the Right, is it not as we said? Colonies regained to this Country by our Moderation, regained with their Loyalty, their Affections and their Trade.

The letter goes on and on in that vein, officiously directing the manner in which the Americans should react. "If you have a Mind to *do Credit to your Friends and strengthen the hands of your Advocates*; hasten, we beseech you to express filial Duty, and Gratitude to your Parent Country." On the other hand,

if [the repeal] is talked of as a Victory, if it is said the Parliament have yielded up the Right, then indeed your Enemies here will have a Complete Triumph. *Your Friends must certainly lose all power to serve you.* Your Tax Masters probably be restored.

The letter is signed by members of the committee, including Trecothick and De Berdt.[15] (Many Americans were incensed by the autocratic tone of the letter.)

Cruger wrote on March 1 to a customer in Rhode Island. "The Stamp Act is not yet repeal'd, but it is as good as done." He gives great credit to "the Merchants and Manufacturers of England. . . . I think you American gentlemen will have all your wishes gratified [and that] the Parliament will never trouble America again."[16]

That more than repeal of the Stamp Act was definitely in the air is shown by this comment in a letter from Edmund Burke to a friend on March 4. "We now prepare for a compleat revision of all the Commercial Laws, which regard our own or the foreign Plantations, from the Act of Navigation downwards." He adds that the "N. Americans and West Indians are now" meeting and soon will have developed "a regular and digested scheme."[17] (The agreement reached on March 10 was important but only a starting point in the negotiations.)

Later in March, Dennys De Berdt wrote two letters about the expected next steps by Parliament. One was to Samuel White, on March 17.

You will have the Molasses duty reduced to 1d & a new Regulation of the Admiralty Courts; a Bill being soon to be brought into the House for that purpose & some other advantages to Trade which will be *supported by the Body of Merchants.*

The other, to William Smith (a member of the governor's council of New York), describes the attitude of the Rockingham ministry.

There is yet much to be done: the Admiralty Courts must be restrained, the exorbitant Duty on Molasses Lowerd, & *the restraints on Trade removed* & this we hope to effect through the favour of the present ministry, who Justly think the Interest of England & Her Colonies one.

De Berdt was overly optimistic. In fact, there will be no relief regarding admiralty courts, nor will restraints on trade be removed.[18]

THE REPEAL

The repeal act (George III c. 11, March 18, 1766) referred to the Stamp Act as being "attended with many inconveniencies, and may be productive of consequences greatly detrimental to the commercial interests of these kingdoms," and is therefore "repealed and made void." It contained no hint of yielding to pressure from the Americans.

Accompanying the repeal—and directly important to the story of the Sugar Act—was the passage of the Declaratory Act (6 George III c. 12, March 18, 1766).

The title:

An act for the better securing the dependency of his majesty's dominions in America upon the crown and parliament of Great Britain.

The preamble. Here is the key element of the act:

[Parliament] had, hath, and of right ought to have, full power and authority to make laws and statutes of sufficient force and validity to bind the colonies and people of America, subjects of the crown of Great Britain, *in all cases whatsoever.*[19]

Its most dramatic feature is the final phrase, "in all cases whatso-ever." Rockingham intended the power and authority to include tax-ation; but, for political reasons, he also intended the statement to be ambiguous. (Given the history of the controversy, the phrase "in all cases" might have been interpreted as "in all cases of legislation," and perhaps excluding taxation.) He even refused specific entreaties to add the word "taxation." Attorney General Charles Yorke insisted that the sentence end: "as well in cases of taxation as in all other cases whatsoever." Rockingham responded on January 25, 1766, that the word "tax" must not appear. "I think I may say that it is our firm resolution in the House of Lords (I mean among ourselves) that that word must not be inserted."[20]

Rockingham's intent that the phrase be ambiguous served a pur-pose in facilitating passage of repeal of the Stamp Act, but had the effect of hiding its true intent—and its importance—from Americans.[21] Deliberations of Parliament in February clarified that the phrase included taxation, but there was no public gallery: no "strangers" were admitted. Although some American agents, mem-bers of the House of Commons, reported the inclusion of taxation, the proceedings were not at first widely known.

Ultimately, the phrase "in all cases whatsoever" was seen by Americans as being obscure; they shrugged off the act as meaningless, perhaps simply an attempt by the British to save face. In any event, the declaration contained nothing specific against which to protest.

NOTIFICATION OF REPEAL

The first notice of the repeal appeared in Boston in a broadside of May 16 and in the *Boston Gazette* on May 19.

From the *London Gazette*.
Westminster, March 18th, 1766
This day his Majesty came to the House of Peers, and being in his royal robes seated on the throne with the usual solemnity . . . was pleased to give his royal assent to an act to repeal [the Stamp Act].

The notice included this item regarding commercial reform.

It is said the Acts of Trade relating to America would be taken

under Consideration, *and all Grievances removed*. The Friends to
America are very powerful, and disposed to assist us to the utmost
of their Ability.[22]

On March 18, the London committee of North American merchants sent another circular letter to correspondents in America. This
version was published in the *Boston Gazette* on June 16, addressed
to prominent patriot "John Hancock Esq; *and the rest of the Merchants in Boston*." On its surface, the purpose of the letter is to simply inform the Americans of the passage of the repeal; but it goes on
to admonish the Americans to "manifest your Gratitude and Affection to your Mother Country, which by the Repeal of this Act has
given such an incontestable proof of her Moderation." They point
out that "you are indebted for this Event to the Clemency and Paternal Regard of his Majesty for the Happiness of his Subjects; to the
Publick Spirit, Abilities, and firmness of the present Administration;
and to the Humanity, prudence and Patriotism [and so on]."[23]

Further demonstration of efforts to shape American policy is a letter of March 18 written at the request of Rockingham. Dr. Thomas
Moffett, an American loyalist in London, wrote Dr. Styles, a patriot
leader in New England. The letter provides an explanation of the situation and an appeal for calm. "If the repeal of the Stamp Act is received in North America with the expected and becoming spirit of
gratitude and obedience really manifested by the restoration of public
and private tranquillity, order and safety," then the friends of America
will continue to have influence in Parliament. Otherwise, if "the
Americans be said to have *conspired in betraying their redeemers, and
even of bringing them to open shame* [then] what the ensuing consequences would be to America and them is but too plain to require any
explanation from me to you." Moffett then exhorts Styles to influence
his friends in America to demonstrate proper gratitude. A confidant
of Grenville's obtained a copy of the letter and provided it to him as
an example of the behind-the-scenes machinations of the Rockingham
ministry to influence the conduct of the Americans. The copy given
to Grenville was annotated with a comment. "This letter is important,
because it shows the arts used by the noble Marquess and his friends
to quiet the Americans after the repeal of the Stamp Act."[24]

On March 31, Secretary of State Conway sent a circular letter to the governors. This is the formal notification of the Declaratory Act and the repeal of the Stamp Act.

> Herewith I have the pleasure of transmitting to You Copies of Two Acts of Parliament just past: The First for securing the just Dependency of the Colonies on the Mother Country: The Second, for the Repeal of the Act of the last Session, granting certain Stamp Duties in America;

Next, he says we have been good to you, now you be good in return.

> The Moderation, the Forbearance, the unexampled Lenity, and Tenderness of Parliament towards the Colonies, which are so signally displayed in those Acts, cannot but dispose the Province committed to your Care to that Return of chearful Obedience to the Laws, and legislative Authority of Great Britain, and to those Sentiments of respectful Gratitude to the mother Country, which are the natural, and, I trust, will be the certain Effects of so much Grace and Condescension, so remarkably manifested on the Part of His Majesty, and of the Parliament; and [on and on for two more paragraphs].

Conway promises to take care of other objections.

> *A Revision of the late American Trade Laws is going to be the immediate Object of Parliament.* Nor will the late Transactions there [i.e., the violent resistance in America], however provoking, prevent I dare say the full operation of that kind and indulgent disposition prevailing both in his Majesty and his Parliament to give to the Trade and Interests of America *every relief which the true State of their circumstances demands.*[25]

REACTION TO THE RETREAT

Later assessments of what occurred in the first half of 1766 (including development and passage of the final incarnation of the Sugar Act, dealt with in the next chapter) provide insight into an interval of calm that characterized the last half of 1766.

American View

American leaders were not entirely insensitive to the need to be supportive of their friends in Parliament, but the admonitions, suggestions, and pleas of the merchants, colonial agents, and friends did not have the desired effect. Americans (despite the perfunctory gratitude expressed by some colonial legislatures) celebrated the repeal with gusto, with jubilant celebration, even overtones of victory. Opposition to British policies continued as vigorously as ever. However, missing from American objections to other British policies was any significant protest to the Declaratory Act.

Samuel Adams (looking back from 1769) provides his reason for the absence of an American protest to the Declaratory Act, despite what he sees (perhaps only in hindsight) as a clear understanding of its meaning.

> As a condition of the repeal, the friends of the American cause . . . were oblig'd to yield to a proposal; that an act should be passed expressly declaring a right in the King, Lords and Commons of Great Britain to make laws which shall be binding on the colonies in all cases whatever.

He claims that Americans "clearly understood the true intention of the words, in all cases whatever, and that a right of making revenue laws binding on the colonies was necessarily included." However:

> The Americans, *for the sake of restoring harmony*, chose to treat this act with silence, at least till necessity should oblige them to remonstrate the ill effects of it.[26]

In 1774, the First Continental Congress gave this similar reason for the lack of protest.

> After the repeal of the Stamp Act, having again resigned ourselves to our ancient and unsuspicious affections for the parent State, and *anxious to avoid any controversy* with her, in hopes of a favourable alteration in sentiments and measures toward us, we *did not press our objections* against [the several] Statutes made subsequent to that repeal.[27]

British View

The British retreat satisfied what Rockingham had seen as the immediate need to end the controversy over trade and taxation, but many British officials—the opposition—remained dissatisfied.

On June 21, 1766, Grenville wrote a friend about his feelings.

> I have not the least doubt that our brethren in America will express great joy at the repeal of the Stamp Act, especially if they understand by it, *as they justly may*, notwithstanding the Declaratory Bill passed at the same time, that they are thereby *exempted for ever from being taxed* by Great Britain for the public support even of themselves.[28]

In 1768, in an essay reflecting the beliefs of the Grenville faction, British subminister William Knox (previously an agent for Georgia) complained of the obsequiousness shown by the Rockingham ministry in 1766. As a result of American resistance in 1765, "a popular cry was, in consequence, raised in this country, for granting the demands of the American subjects."

> The mischiefs to be apprehended from a refusal were so much exaggerated, their strength to resist so roundly asserted, that parliament gave into the imposition, and *gave up the taxes without requiring an acknowledgment from the colonies of its supremacy*, or their making compensation to the revenue by any grants of their provincial assemblies.

Relevant to the Sugar Act regulations:

> The restraints which had been laid upon their trade by some late acts of parliament, and still more by the strict execution of the old laws, they complained had disabled them from making specie remittances to England; and parliament and ministry seemed to vie with each other in giving credit to their representations, and in removing obstructions to the freedom of American commerce.

Overall, the essay was a defense of actions taken by the Grenville administration, including praise for the Sugar Act. "The American colonies . . . had no military establishment of their own; and, as Great-Britain furnished them with troops, they were required to supply her with revenue for their payment." In addition, "The "laws of trade were carried into strict execution, and clandestine importations universally checked."[29]

PART THREE

Duties for Revenue

"Resolved. The following acts of parliament are infringements and violations of the rights of the colonists; and that the repeal of them is essentially necessary, in order to restore harmony between Great Britain and the American colonies, viz.: The several acts of 4 Geo. III. ch. 15 . . . 6 Geo. III. ch. 52 . . . which impose duties for the purpose of raising a revenue in America . . . are subversive of American rights."
—First Continental Congress, 1774

Seven

The Sugar Act of 1766

"That a Duty of One Penny, Sterling Money, per Gallon, be laid upon all Melasses and Syrups, which shall be imported into such British Colony or Plantation."
— House of Commons, May 9, 1766

"Every grievance of which you complained, is now absolutely and totally removed—a joyful and happy event for the late disconsolate inhabitants of America."
— An American agent, May 15, 1766

FOLLOWING REPEAL OF THE STAMP ACT, THE NEXT ISSUE TAKEN up by the Rockingham ministry was reform of commercial legislation. That is, deal with American requests that Parliament reverse expanded jurisdiction of admiralty courts, remove undue burdens on trade, and end or reduce the duty on foreign molasses. The Sugar Act of 1766 was the primary British response to those protests.[1] It did satisfy the grievance regarding the oppressively burdensome and long-complained-of molasses duty, but was otherwise unresponsive to American grievances (in fact, placing further restrictions on colonial trade).

The Sugar Act of 1766 was the first act of Parliament dealing with America that was unambiguous in its use of customs duties to raise revenue. As the most important example, the previous dual-purpose molasses duty was transformed into a straightforward tax, equally levied on foreign and British molasses. Oddly however, perhaps as an aftereffect from many years of seeing the Sugar Act as regulation of trade, Americans continued to look at the molasses duty and other duties of the act as trade regulation, making no protest about taxation. As a consequence—a factor not immediately obvious and that took years to play out—the act fulfilled the British desire to exact significant revenue from America.

HOW THE ACT CAME ABOUT

Even before final action on repeal of the Stamp Act, the principal interested parties came to an understanding about commercial reform. The kickoff was, "A meeting of the Committees of the West Indian and North American Merchants at the King's Arms Tavern 10th March 1766." Not all the agreements survived later negotiation, but the meeting was nonetheless important as an initial instance of cooperation. A key agreement was *that the Duty on the foreign Molasses imported into North America be reduced to one penny Sterling per Gallon and that every possible method be adopted to enforce the full and just collection of that Duty."*[2]

On March 12, Rockingham informed the king that he had received

> a deputation from the Committee of N. America & from the West India Island Committee this morning, who came to inform him that several of the Matters which might have occasioned dispute were nearly agreed between them. Lord Rockingham has now full Reason to assure his Majesty that there is the Greatest Prospect of an Advantageous System of Commerce being established for the Mutual & General Interest of this Country, N. America, and the West India Islands.[3]

The American Committee of the House of Commons met at length in March and April, hearing testimony and debating issues related to the Sugar Act of 1764. The testimony of the merchants went on hour after hour, often with observations that the duty on molasses raises the price of rum. "This Act of 1764 . . . affects the Guinea trade by raising the price of the rum which our merchants sell on the coast of Africa, and by this means they cannot meet the foreign merchants upon so good a footing."[4] The Grenville faction consistently resisted the program of the Rockingham ministry. Edmund Burke wrote a friend on April 24 that "we are, it is true, demolishing the whole Grenvillian Fabrick . . . but too much I fear will remain in spite of all our Labours."[5]

In the committee on April 30, Chancellor of the Exchequer William Dowdeswell made a number of proposals including "reducing the duty on foreign molasses from 3d. a gallon to one penny per gallon." William Beckford answered him; he "was strongly in opposition to the penny duty on molasses, saying it was beneficial to North America and the French, but prejudicial to Great Britain and our Sugar Islands." His reasoning was "that making molasses cheaper would ... enable the French to sell sugar cheaper by finding a mart for their molasses, which otherwise they must throw away." Grenville also spoke against the one-penny duty, "that 2d. was the lowest the Americans themselves had proposed; that a penny per gallon and five farthings was what they usually paid for cheating." As part of his discussion, Grenville criticized the ministry and the process of decision-making, complaining of their "taking off tax after tax upon evidence at the Bar ex parte only," then scathingly objecting to "delegation of administration to a *Club of North America merchants* at the King's Arms Tavern."[6]

On May 9, the American Committee reported to the House of Commons fourteen resolutions made the previous day. The resolutions of the American Committee took into account the agreements made earlier that day in the smaller West Indian Committee. Of special importance to the Sugar Act story is, "Agreement of the West Indian Committee. Endorsed House of Commons, May 8th. 1766." It included the remarkable resolution that a duty of "1d per Gallon be laid upon Melasses of the British Sugar Colonies imported into North America."[7]

In consequence, the American Committee resolutions included:

[1] That the Duties imposed, by any Act or Acts of Parliament, upon [foreign] Melasses, and Syrups . . . imported into any British Colony or Plantation in America, do cease and determine [i.e., terminate].

The following resolve amounts to a change of policy—an inadvertent change of policy.

[2] That a Duty of One Penny, Sterling Money, per Gallon, be laid upon all Melasses and Syrups, which shall be imported into such British Colony or Plantation.[8]

The phrasing is important, stating *all molasses*, later appearing in the act with the phrase *British as well as foreign*. Levy of the duty on British molasses at the same rate as that charged on foreign molasses transformed the duty into a straightforward tax. First of all, there being no reason other than revenue for having a duty on British molasses, it was simply a tax. Secondly, the duty on foreign molasses—previously wearing the fig leaf of a preferential tariff—lost its status as a trade regulation, and was similarly simply a tax.

The change in the nature of the molasses duty is of considerable importance, affecting the nature of the Sugar Act, and informing British opinion about American acceptance of external taxation. British leaders did not plan this transformation; there was no intent to so explicitly levy this tax. Although there was early agreement to reduce the duty on foreign molasses to one penny (a rate acceptable to American merchants), the new levy of a one-penny duty on molasses from the British islands came out of the give-and-take of committee meetings.

The treating of British molasses in a manner identical to foreign molasses was a remarkable concession on the part of the West Indian interests, abandoning the pretense that the duty was important to protection of their molasses exports. (The change was of no significance regarding revenue or the flow of trade, with little molasses being exported from British sugar islands to America in any event.) Helping to prompt the concession was that British plantations were dependent on imported provisions. "Since the West Indies depended upon the mainland for their food-supply, it was the threat of an anti-exportation agreement" by the Americans that influenced their attitude toward negotiation. In addition, the West Indian interests received important consideration regarding duties on British sugar, and regarding the treatment of sugar imported to Great Britain via

North America. As a consequence, "the West Indians did not consider the compromise in the light of a defeat." Looking at the change from a different point of view, Rose Fuller wrote the (now ageing but still politically important) Duke of Newcastle the very next day about an advantage to Great Britain, pointing out that a reduction of the duty on foreign molasses from three pence to one penny per gallon, along with making the duty applicable to molasses from the British sugar islands, might be an improvement. It is a duty "which will certainly be collected [and] will also accustom the North American Colonies to obedience."[9]

All fourteen resolutions from the American Committee were approved. Agent Joseph Sherwood reported to Rhode Island Governor Ward on May 15.

> The House, on the 9th instant, agreed with their committee on the following resolutions: by which, you will see that *every grievance of which you complained, is now absolutely and totally removed*—a joyful and happy event for the late disconsolate inhabitants of America. I trust they will make a wise and prudent use of the tender indulgences shown them by their now affectionate mother.[10]

Sherwood quoted from the resolves, but made no special mention of the fact that the one-penny duty was to be laid on British molasses as well as foreign. In fact, and more generally, the change in the nature of the duty went unremarked, virtually overlooked, with neither the British nor the Americans making any particular note of its relationship to taxation; or to American rights; or to the authority of Parliament.

On May 10, the committee on ways and means reported additional resolutions (duly approved), including this new condition that became a major grievance of the Americans.

> That all sugars which shall be imported into this Kingdom, from any British Colony or Plantation *on the Continent of America*, be made subject to the like Duties as are now payable upon the Importation of French Sugars.[11]

Another topic of negotiation was the establishment of free ports in the West Indies. The result was a Free Port Act, also passed in 1766.[12] Although contrary to the interests of Americans, it was not a noteworthy grievance; and although part of Rockingham's plan for commercial reform, free ports have little mention in the Sugar Act text.

TEXT OF THE ACT

The Sugar Act of 1766 (6 George III c. 52)[13] amended the Sugar Act of 1764.

The title:

> An act for repealing certain duties, in the British colonies and plantations, granted by several acts of parliament . . . and for granting other duties instead thereof; and for further encouraging, regulating, and securing, several branches of the trade of this kingdom, and the British dominions in America.

The preamble:

> Whereas the several duties herein after mentioned, imposed by certain acts of parliament to be raised in the British colonies and plantations in America, have been attended with great inconveniencies to the trade of his Majesty's dominions; and it is therefore necessary that the same should be discontinued, and that other duties *should be granted in lieu thereof*: we, your Majesty's most dutiful and loyal subjects, the commons of Great Britain in parliament assembled, do therefore most humbly beseech your Majesty, that it may be enacted . . .

Nowhere in the title or preamble of the 1766 act is there a whiff of taxation, but the phrases of 1764 indicating taxation (giving and granting, raising a revenue) although not explicitly stated, were implicitly still part of the Sugar Act. (In October 1774 the First Continental Congress had this to say: "In this Statute, the Commons, *avoiding the terms of giving and granting*, 'humbly besought his Majesty, that it might be enacted, &c.' But from a declaration in the preamble, that the rates and duties were 'in lieu of' several others granted by the Statute first before mentioned for raising a revenue, and from some other expressions it appears, that *these duties were intended for that purpose.*"[14])

The remainder of the preamble repeals several duties. First is specification of the molasses duty to be repealed.

That all the duties imposed by any act or acts of parliament upon *melasses or syrups* of the growth, product, or manufacture, of any *foreign American colony or plantation* imported into any British colony or plantation in America;

Next is specification of sugar duties to be repealed. (These are the duties established in 1673 on "Sugar, White" and "Browne Sugar and Muscavadoes.")

and also the duties imposed by an act made in the twenty fifth year of the reign of King Charles the Second . . . upon sugar of the growth, production, and manufacture, of the British plantations in America, which should be laden there.

This was advantageous for the West Indian interests, widening the differential between British and foreign sugar imported into America—a reward for cooperation on other issues during the negotiations. (Ironically, it was these plantation duties that motivated in 1730 the initial recommendation for duties on the importation of foreign sugar into America.)

The preamble also specifies the 1764 export duties on coffee from the British plantations. Finally, all the duties specified, shall "cease, determine, and be no longer paid."

Sections 2 and 3 repeal additional duties, with little effect on American commerce.

Section 4 establishes the lower molasses duty without specifying foreign colonies. This quietly levies what turns out to be a source of revenue greater than that from any other such du, product: an unambiguous tax that, for a number of years, was paid by American merchants with little complaint.

IV. And be it further enacted . . . there shall be raised, levied, collected, and paid . . . the several and respective rates and duties herein after mentioned;

For every gallon (wine-measure) of melasses and syrups, which shall be imported or brought . . . into any colony or plantation in America, which now is, or hereafter may be, under the dominion of his Majesty, his heirs, and successors, *one penny.*

This section also reinstates the duty on British coffee, and causes the duty to be collected on importation rather than exportation.

For every hundred weight avoirdupois of coffee, of the growth and produce of any British colony or plantation in America, which shall be imported or brought from thence into any other British colony or plantation in America, seven shillings.

Sections 5 through 11, largely regulations about fabrics, had little effect on American commerce. Section 12 deals with payment ("sterling money of Great Britain") and use of revenue from specified goods, stating the same purpose as the act of 1764.

XII. That all the monies that shall arise by the said duties charged by this act upon melasses and syrups, coffee . . . [shall be appropriated] towards defraying the necessary expenses of defending, protecting, and securing the British colonies and plantations in America.

I skip over a lengthy description of regulations, including exemption from duties for certain goods, and for those warehoused under close control of customs officers and then re-exported to Britain: e.g., British coffee, foreign sugars and coffee, cotton wool, tea, cocoa nuts, and chocolate. Of those, section 16 merits comment. The point of the section is that certain foreign goods, sugar being by far the most important, shall be free of duty when imported to America, provided they are warehoused and re-exported within twelve months. Regulations regarding exportation varied by product. For sugar, it was to be exported only to Great Britain or to Europe south of Cape Finisterre (southern Europe).

Section 23 deals with sugar imported into Great Britain. It starts with the new policy of treating all sugar exported from North America as French sugar, even if it was originally from British sugar islands.

> XXIII. And it is hereby further enacted [that] all sugars which shall be imported into Great Britain, from any part of the British colonies or plantations *on the continent of America*, shall be deemed and taken to be French sugars.

This became a major grievance of American merchants. An important component of American trade with British sugar plantations had long been return cargoes of sugar for reshipping to Great Britain: previously, British-grown sugar imported to Britain from North America was treated in the same manner as that imported from the British West Indies. Despite the resulting disruption to American commerce, from the British point of view the regulation was necessary in order to end the practice of smuggling foreign sugar into America, and then exporting it with the claim that it was British. Section 23 further requires that the importer must pay "three pence per hundred weight avoirdupois for such sugars, which shall not be afterwards drawn back or repaid upon the exportation of the same goods." Other import duties on this sugar are deferred "provided such sugars upon landing, be immediately lodged and secured under the King's locks, in warehouses provided at the sole expence of the importer." Then, if the sugars are exported outside the empire, no further duty is levied. Sections 24 through 27 add additional regulations regarding such sugars.

Section 28 deals with receipt of duties from goods not specified in section 12, including "duties hereby also imposed upon sugars imported [into Great Britain] from any British colony or plantation on the continent of America, as shall exceed the duties now payable upon sugar so imported." Such funds "shall be, from time to time, paid into the receipt of his Majesty's exchequer distinctly and apart from all other branches of the public revenue." Such funds are not specifically appropriated, but simply reserved "for the disposition of parliament."

Section 29 repeals as no longer necessary special restrictions on shipping molasses, particularly the burdensome requirement in the act of 1764 that bond must be given, before goods are loaded, for the situation "in case any [foreign] molasses or syrups" are later brought on board. The section makes a lengthy restatement of regulations to be repealed, then:

> XXIX. And whereas the Duty upon foreign Melasses or Syrups imported into the British Colonies in America are now reduced; and all Melasses and Syrups, *British as well as foreign*, are made subject to the same Duty; be it therefore enacted [that] so much of the said recited acts as relate to any proof or certificate . . . or any bond to be entered into with respect to foreign melasses or syrups, shall be, and the same is hereby declared to be, repealed.

The relief afforded American merchants and masters of vessels provided by section 29 is undone by section 30; it imposes more extensive bond requirements than does the provision repealed. The section starts by alluding to existing statutes that deal with *enumerated goods*, which "shall be brought by such ship or vessel to some other British plantation, or to some port in Great Britain." The stated concern of this section is to prevent the illicit shipping of such enumerated goods on ships that clear out as carrying only non-enumerated goods. In addition, there is a need to prevent such ships from clandestinely bringing a return cargo of European products (the primary concern being manufactured goods that were required to be imported only from Great Britain).

> XXX. Now, in order more effectually to prevent such [enumerated] Goods being privately carried from any British Colony or Plantation in America into foreign parts of Europe in vessels that clear out with non-enumerated goods, as well as to prevent the clandestine Importation of foreign European goods into the said British Colonies; be it further enacted [that from January 1, 1767] bond and security . . . shall also be given to the collector . . . at any port or place in any of the British American colonies or plantations.

The bond must be given by

the master of *every ship or vessel* that shall lade or take on board there any goods not particularly enumerated in the said acts with condition, that such goods shall not be landed at any part of Europe to the northward of Cape Finisterre, except in Great Britain.[15]

Section 31 clarifies the intent of section 30, that it does not apply to "Ports of Spain within the Bay of Biscay."

In summary, bond must be given to guarantee that non-enumerated goods "shall not be landed" in northern Europe and—as required by previous acts—enumerated goods "shall be brought" to a British port. The mandate is broad: bonds are required for *every ship or vessel*, any size, decked or undecked, even for coastal traffic within the same colony. As a practical matter, exemption was often granted to small vessels engaged exclusively in coastal and river trade, but the words of the act did not allow this, giving great discretion to customs officers (sometime inappropriately used to harass legal traders).

In addition to reestablishing the onerous bonding requirement, sections 30 and 31 establish, for the first time, a thorough prohibition of direct trade with northern Europe, the manufacturing countries in competition with Great Britain. Henceforth, non-enumerated goods to be exported to northern Europe must be unladen in a British port, then reloaded for re-export. The prohibition includes such previously unrestricted goods as wheat, fish, beef, and dairy products.

The new restriction on trade was a major disruption to existing trade routes, and generated much American protest, particularly in regard to trade with Ireland. That restriction was lifted the next year by 7 George III c. 2. The actionable phrases in that act are, "and whereas Ireland should have been excepted in the said act as well as Great Britain," such goods "may be landed in Ireland." The title of the act lifting the restriction is suggestive of the complex nature of the laws of trade (and the Sugar Act), beginning with a purpose of amending the act of 1766. "An act to amend so much of an act made in the last Session of parliament, intituled, An act for repealing certain duties, in the British colonies and plantations . . ."[16]

Thomas Jefferson thought the regulations so troublesome that in 1774 he included this comment in his *Summary View of the Rights of British America*. In objecting to the claimed "uncontrouled power" of Parliament to establish regulations, he protested that, in addition to duties imposed, regulations prohibit

> our going to any markets northward of cape Finesterre, in the kingdom of Spain, for the sale of commodities which Great Britain will not take from us, and for the purshase of others, with which she cannot supply us, and that for no other than the arbitrary purpose of [advantage to Great Britain at a severe cost to the colonies].[17]

The final section 32 repeats the 1764 protection for customs officers against suit by the merchant or master of a vessel seized.

The act passed Commons on May 30, Lords a few days later (without a division in either house), and received the royal assent on June 6, 1766, the final day for that session of Parliament. In closing, the king made this comment about the commercial regulations.

> The many Regulations which you have made, for extending and promoting the Trade and Manufactures of Great Britain, and for settling the mutual Intercourse of My Kingdoms and Plantations, in such a Manner as to provide for the Improvement of the Colonies on a *Plan of due Subordination to the Commercial Interests of the Mother Country*, are the strongest Proofs of your equitable and comprehensive Regard to the Welfare of all My Dominions; an Object truly worthy of a British Parliament.[18]

COMPLEXITY OF THE REGULATIONS

Trade regulations were so complex, involving multiple acts of Parliament, that special instructions were prepared for British officials at American ports. For example, *The Acts of Trade and Navigation in Force February 1769* (a printed forty-page document) was issued under the authority of "the Commissioners of His Majesty's Customs in America." It integrates and references not only the Sugar Act, but the many exceptions and modifications made in other acts. Here is an extract from the instructions for an officer of the customs.

You are to take notice that all goods and commodities of the growth, produce, or manufacture of the British Colonies are distinguished as enumerated and non-enumerated.

The restriction on enumerated goods is where they *shall be landed*.

The enumerated consisting of [24 items] are not to be laden on board of *any vessel* until the master with one surety shall enter into a bond . . . with condition that the said goods *shall be landed in* some British Colony, or in Great-Britain, under a forfeiture of the said goods and vessel.

The restriction on non-enumerated goods is where they shall *not* be landed.

The non-enumerated goods, consisting of all other goods or commodities of the growth, produce or manufacture of the British Colonies, are not to be loaded on board of *any vessel* until the master with one surety hath entered into the like bond . . . conditional that the said goods *shall not be carried* to any part of Europe, northward of Cape-Finisterre, except to Great-Britain or Ireland, under forfeiture of such goods and vessel.[19]

The instructions reinforce the troublesome requirement for giving bond before loading goods, and continue to state, incorrectly, that the regulations apply to *any vessel*—despite the corrective action (as I noted in chapter 4) of 5 George III c. 45 that exempted local commerce in "boats or small vessels without decks which do not go to open sea." The resulting discretion given to customs officers opened the door to unequal treatment of merchants.[20]

NEWS TO AMERICA

On June 12, the Duke of Richmond, secretary of state, wrote the American governors. He included this upbeat view of accomplishments of the ministry.

Those Grievances in Trade which seemed to be the first and chief Object of [American] Uneasiness, have been taken into the most minute Consideration & such Regulations have been established, as will, it is hoped, restore the Trade of America, not only to its former flourishing State, but be the means of greatly encreasing & improving it to the Conveniency & Advantage of all His Majesty's Subjects, in every Part of His Dominions.[21]

On June 13, the London committee of North American merchants sent another circular letter to correspondents in America. The letter to Boston was addressed to John Hancock, and published in the *Boston Gazette*, September 8. It starts with a referral to the letters we saw in chapter 6.

Refering you to our former Letters of 28th Febry and 18th March, both of which we hope you have long since receiv'd, we now inclose [among others, the Sugar Act of 1766]. We consider [these acts] as the basis of an extensive System of Trade between Great Britain and her Colonies framed on liberal principles of reciprocal Advantage, *relieving the Colonies from injudicious restrictions and severe Duties.*

The letter then reinforces the importance of ending illicit trade with "the manufacturing Countries of Europe." In order "that your Friends here will not on any future occasion be made to blush by instances of its violation," the colonies must comply with "the Clause of the regulation Act [i.e., Sugar Act of 1766] inhibiting that intercourse." They reinforce all the above with this restatement of the guiding principle between Great Britain and the colonies.

In a word, the System of Great Britain is to promote a mutual interest by Supplying the Colonies with her Manufactures, by encouraging them to raise, and receiving from them all raw materials, and by granting the largest extension to every branch of their Trade not interfering with her own.[22]

END OF A MINISTRY

The end of this part of the story also sees the end of the Rockingham administration, after almost exactly one year in office. In the summer of 1766, the ministry changed for complicated political and personal reasons (having little to do with the situation in America). Rockingham was dismissed and replaced by William Pitt, soon made Lord Chatham. Rockingham, insistent on claiming that his ministry had been a success, summarized the situation in America during his final meeting with the king on July 9.

> By the last accounts from America, the Repeal of the Stamp Act had had all the good effect, that could be proposed; *had been received with the utmost duty, and gratitude*; and that everything was quiet in America and not one mark left of disobedience, or discontent.[23]

In August, Edmund Burke published a pamphlet (a bit of political propaganda) justifying the Rockingham administration: *A Short Account of a Late Short Administration.*

> The trade of America was set free from injudicious and ruinous impositions—its revenue was improved, and settled upon a rational foundation—its commerce extended with foreign countries; while all the advantages were secured to Great Britain, by the [Sugar Act of 1766].[24]

The situation in America may not have been as bright as expressed by Rockingham and Burke, but the last half of the year was largely marked by comity and goodwill. Here is another upbeat observation.

> After great perturbations for two years and a half, with little interruption, there was a *short space of tranquillity*. Besides the repeal of the stamp act, the duty on molasses had been reduced from three-pence to one penny per gallon; and encouragement had been given to expect a revisal, and favourable alteration, of several acts of parliament which restrain the commerce of the colonies. . . . Thus stood affairs in Massachusetts Bay at the close of the year 1766.[25]

Although protests were quieted, any expectations of commercial reform went unmet.

RESPONSE TO SUGAR ACT DUTIES

At the end of 1766 the Sugar Act story splits into divergent paths, the Americans exhibiting contradictory responses to the duties imposed. The first, a story I will tell in this chapter, is that (despite protest to the lack of commercial reform) Americans comply with the act and pay its duties. The second story deals with American rejection of taxation and demand for repeal of the Sugar Act. The latter story is deferred to the following two chapters.

Commercial Problems Not Resolved

In the long run, American objections to the Sugar Act centered on unconstitutional taxation. But it is useful to investigate one protest shortly after passage of the act of 1766, demonstrating that it failed to satisfy American commercial objections.

On November 28, 1766, 240 merchants of New York City submitted a petition addressed to the House of Commons (via the Board of Trade and Secretary of State Shelburne). First, a preamble.

> The commerce of the North American colonies is so severely clogged and restricted by the *statutes of the 4th and 6th of his present majesty's reign,* as to afford a melancholy presage of its destruction, the fatal effects of which [and so on] they think it their duty to implore the house to resume the consideration of the plantation trade, for effectual redress.

The petition repeats arguments we have seen ever since early 1764. Imports from foreign islands were necessary

> to supply the various branches of their trade [otherwise] the petitioners must be plunged into a total incapacity of making good their payments of British debts; their credit must sink, and their imports from Great Britain gradually diminish [and so on] which will be attended with consequences very detrimental to those of Great Britain.

The petition even further emphasizes "that sugar, rum, melasses . . . are the essentials of their return cargoes" from trade with the foreign islands. It is particularly important that sugar be a profitable trade item.

The heavy embarrassments which attend the article of sugar, is a capital subject of complaint . . . it often happens *that at the foreign islands a sufficient return-cargo independent of sugar, cannot be procured*, which renders trade precarious and discouraging.

The duty on foreign unrefined sugar was a major problem.

The high duty of 5s. sterling a hundred, is found by experience to be so excessive, that it has induced the fair trader to decline that branch of business, while, to people less scrupulous, it presents an irresistible temptation to smuggling.

"The petitioners therefore most humbly entreat that a more moderate duty be laid on foreign sugars." And further,

The compelling merchants to land and store foreign sugars in Great Britain, before they are exported to other parts of Europe, is another expensive and dilatory restriction, without being of any material advantage to the revenue of Great Britain.

The act of 1766 has created another problem.

That British plantation sugar exported from North America, should be declared French on being landed in England, the petitioners conceive may be justly classed among the number of hardships inflicted by those regulations, as in effect it deprives them of making a remittance in that article, by exposing them to the payment of the foreign duty in Great Britain, which appears the more severe, as their fellow-subjects of the islands are left at liberty to export those sugars for what they really are.

The petition switches to suggesting a new duty, "a moderate duty," on imported rum (but not French rum), as it would "would add considerably to the revenue, prevent smuggling," and provide other benefits.

After noting British failure to resolve other problems—including "the jurisdiction of the admiralty" and the restrictions regarding trade with the wine-producing islands (which hamper export of "wheat, flour, fish, and lumber")—the petition reaches the core issue.

> Although, at the last session, the necessity of relieving the trade
> of these Colonies seems to have been universally admitted, *never-*
> *theless*, experience has evinced, that the commercial regulations
> then enacted, *instead of remedying, have increased the heavy bur-*
> *then under which it already laboured.*

The petition goes on and on with other grievances and suggestions
for relief, ending with, "The petitioners, therefore, pray the house to
take the above into consideration and to grant such relief therein
[and so on]."[26]

Thomas Pownall, a member of the House of Commons who made
American affairs his primary public interest, and was earlier (1757-
59) the governor of Massachusetts Bay, later praised the document
in his widely respected *The Administration of the British Colonies*.
"The matters . . . are fairly stated, according to the truth and fact;
and the consequences thence deduced, are such as actual experience
shows to be in existence; I am sure I cannot give a more clear, distinct,
or better state of the American commerce than it contains."[27]

Massachusetts also submitted a petition (sent to agent De Berdt,
January 17, 1767) as a "representation of the difficulties which Trade
still labors under by means of some late Acts of Parliament." Boston
merchants had been prompted by a letter of November 24, 1766,
from the New York merchants saying that "the universal and con-
current opinions of the principal merchants through the Continent,
all uniting in material points, must carry conviction."[28]

The New York and Massachusetts protests were only one manifestation of deeper discontent. Governor Bernard wrote Secretary of
State Shelburne on December 22, 1766, reporting that he saw no reduction in radical reaction to British policy. "The repeal [of the
Stamp Act] occasioned no relaxation in the disposition and designs
of the faction which had raised itself by the Act."

> Mr. Otis at a meeting at the Town Hall (which I think was to fix a
> time for public rejoicings for the repeal) in a set Speech told the Peo-
> ple that "*the distinction between inland taxes & port duties was*

without foundation; for whoever had a right to impose one had a right to impose the other: & therefore as the Parliament had given up the one (for he said the Act for securing the dependency [i.e., the Declaratory Act] had no relation to taxes) *they had given up the other*; & the Merchants were great fools, if they submitted any longer to the Laws restraining their Trade, which ought to be free."[29]

The suggestion that "Parliament had given up" the right to tax the colonies and that merchants should ignore restraints on their trade represents the sort of attitude that Grenville had predicted would result from repeal of the Stamp Act.

An exchange of letters in early February 1767 gives a hint of British displeasure. First, Secretary of State Shelburne to Lord Chatham. In addition to other ongoing controversy, "a petition is at the same time come from New York, signed by two hundred and forty persons, to the House of Commons, and sent to the Board of Trade to present." Chatham responded two days later. "America affords a gloomy prospect. . . . The petition of the merchants of New York is highly improper; in point of time most absurd; in the extent of their pretensions most excessive, and in the reasoning most grossly fallacious and offensive."[30] The petition was read in the House of Commons on February 16, thereafter ignored.

The Massachusetts petition avoided such ignominious treatment. De Berdt wrote the Boston merchants on March 9, 1767.

> I duly received your obliging favour of the 17 Jany accompanying a Pettition to the House of Commons, which I shall Tomorrow lay before Lord Shelburn.
>
> The New York Pettition had some warm [expressions] which gave offence to the House [i.e., on February 16] & the Pettition was orderd to lay on the Table.

On March 14, he reported that he "waited on Lord Shelburne with your Petition" but that he was advised not "to push it just at this juncture when the Enemies of America are so numerous, and the House very much offended at the Conduct of New York." De Berdt followed that good advice.[31]

Americans Accept Taxation

American merchants treated the molasses duty as a regulation of trade levied at a reasonable rate, with the result that they acquiesced, they paid the duty (and other Sugar Act duties), finally fulfilling the British goal of drawing significant revenue from America. There is no simple reason why Americans paid the tax on molasses with little complaint, but acceptance started with the Americans getting what they asked for: a low rate of duty. Beyond that, it is less clear why the Americans were quiet.

One likely explanation for lack of protest is that merchants had a long history of thinking about the duty as a regulation of trade, the high rate being the only grievance. In 1766, the duty having been reduced to the level they had long desired, there was no reason to complain. (The extra duty paid on molasses imported from British sugar islands was inconsequential.) It was easy to overlook the constitutional issue that it had become a tax.[32]

In the long run, there was little protest because any discontent about a molasses tax became lost in the enmity raised by a new set of taxes imposed in 1767 (which we will see in the next chapter). A final reason for lack of protest is the very nature of the Sugar Act; it conflated taxation with regulation, making protest appear to be an attack on the Navigation Acts. Any attack on the near-sacred laws of trade would antagonize the ministry, the king, and both houses of Parliament. British taxpayers, already heavily burdened, would end up paying any amount not exacted from Americans. As a consequence, it was difficult to put pressure on British friends of America for a repeal of the taxation clauses.

Sugar Act Revenue

Let's take a detailed look at the revenue obtained by the British from the Sugar Act. The amount of revenue collected as duties paid is not as important as the fact that it was collected without protest, but it does drive home that revenue resulting from the act was substantial.[33] Table 6-1 summarizes that revenue.[34]

It is useful to pay special attention to the years 1768 to 1772, as these are the years for which the most accurate revenue data are available for both the Sugar Act and other parliamentary revenues.

TABLE 6-1. Sugar Act Revenues, 1765-1774 (£ Sterling)

Year	Molasses	Sugar	Madeira	British Coffee, Other	Sugar Act
1765					14,091
1766					26,696
1767					33,844
1768	11,927	4,145	7,000	1,318	24,659
1769	18,488	12,836	6,510	2,104	39,938
1770	15,103	8,759	5,341	1,707	30,910
1771	15,806	5,269	4,872	1,139	27,086
1772	20,328	14,055	6,055	2,132	42,570
1773					39,531
1774					27,074
Total	81,652	45,064	29,778	8,400	306,399

TABLE 6-2. Summary Revenue for the Sugar Act: 1768-1772

Molasses	£82
Sugar	£45
Madeira	£30
British Coffee, Other	£8
Total for Sugar Act	£165

Table 6-2 provides a summary version of Sugar Act revenue for those years, rounded to thousands of pounds sterling.[35]

For those five years the Sugar Act accounted for 82 percent of all money collected by British customs.[36] The molasses duty produced half of all the Sugar Act revenue; most of the remaining was also primarily taxation.

In addition to revenue, the effect of the act on avenues of trade validated contentions that the trade in foreign molasses was necessary to meet American needs. For those same five years, the average annual importation of molasses was four million gallons, almost all of which (all but 3 percent) was from the foreign islands.[37]

The Sugar Act of 1766 was ostensibly intended to satisfy American demands for commercial reform, but in fact offered little relief other than reduction of the molasses duty. The reduction in the duty, although having the not-so-obvious effect of transforming the molasses duty into a straightforward tax, mollified American merchants, leading to an end of protests about duties of the Sugar Act. Indeed, since Americans complied with the act—and paid the duties—it became the most successful act of parliamentary taxation implemented in America, the exception to "no taxation without representation."[38]

In addition, the molasses duty being transformed into a tax had an unanticipated consequence: American acceptance of this tax reinforced the British belief that American constitutional objections did not apply to port duties.

Eight

A Distinction Without
a Difference

"The colonies submit to pay all external taxes laid on them by way of duty on merchandizes imported into their country, and never disputed the authority of parliament to lay such duties."
—"Benevolus" (Benjamin Franklin), 1767

"I do not know any distinction between internal and external taxes; it is a distinction without a difference, it is perfect nonsense; if we have a right to impose one, we have the other."
—Charles Townshend, 1767

IN 1767, PARLIAMENT IMPOSED A NEW SET OF TAXES ON COLONIAL trade. British leaders believed that the new taxes, collected as duties at American ports, were consistent with what they saw as American acceptance of external taxes—especially the quiet acceptance of the one-penny duty on all imported molasses. Surprising the British, the Americans viewed the new taxes as being unconstitutional, and resisted. Even further, the new taxation caused the Americans to reassess their view of what was acceptable and what was not; it drove them to stand "against the general principle of raising any revenue in America."

THE UNDERSTANDING HELD BY BRITISH LEADERS

The nature of American protest to the duties of the Sugar Act of 1764, and compliance with the duties of 1766, put British leaders on the road to an understanding that, save for economic problems, the Americans had no objection to revenue being raised by duties: that external taxes were constitutionally acceptable to the colonists.[1]

The ministry assembled by William Pitt, Earl of Chatham, was mixed in attitude toward America. Chatham was often sympathetic to American grievances, but as a consequence of near-constant illness he lost influence and the ministry was adrift. Revenue policy became dominated by Chancellor of the Exchequer Charles Townshend. Here is an illuminating report from Connecticut agent William Samuel Johnson, writing Governor William Pitkin on February 12, 1767.

> It is said the complexion of the Ministry and of Parliament seems rather unfavorable to the Colonies; and it is imagined that new plans are meditating with respect to them, but what they are does not appear. Mr. Townsend, Chancellor of the Exchequer [later characterized by Johnson as "a gentleman of the first abilities, but of extreme instability"], a few days past, upon an accidental mention of America, said in the House, "I do not know any distinction between internal and external taxes; it is a distinction without a difference, it is perfect nonsense; *if we have a right to impose one, we have the other.*"[2]

Townshend is getting into trouble here: the Americans are about ready to agree that there is no difference. It was clear to Americans that Parliament has no right to impose internal taxes; and they are beginning to reason that, if it has *no right* to impose one, it has *no right to impose the other*.

Townshend mentioned the issue again on February 18. "He spoke of the distinction between internal and external taxes as not founded in reason but *proper to be adopted in policy.*" Thomas Whately wrote John Temple on February 25 with a description of the current mood of British leaders. "The tide is entirely turn'd here with respect to America, that the distinction between external & internal taxes is totally exploded, that every doubt upon the right is ridiculed & censured whenever it is mention'd."[3]

John Huske wrote Townshend with his advice on April 9. His opinion carries extra weight since he is both knowledgeable about and generally friendly to America.

> Permit me to remark to you, that it is certain by a regulation of the trade of America for the reciprocal interest of both mother and children, you may have a sufficient revenue to pay all Great Britain's expense for her colonies and in a manner *perfectly agreeable to both under your conduct.*

In a word of caution, Huske continues that his opinion is contingent on, "you give them a currency. Till then you are demanding brick without straw."[4] (He was alluding to action that ought to be taken to relieve problems caused by the *Currency Act* of 1764.)

Benjamin Franklin, writing anonymously as "Benevolus" in the *London Chronicle*, published a lengthy article as subtle support for the colonies. *On the Propriety of Taxing America* was first printed on April 11 (later in other London newspapers, and by June in colonial newspapers, acknowledging the true authorship). Franklin wrote in order to correct what he saw as misconceptions held by those in London, including the idea "that the colonies contend the parliament of Britain has no authority over them." Benevolus makes this emphatic statement.

> The colonies submit to pay all external taxes laid on them by way of duty on merchandizes imported into their country, and never disputed the authority of parliament to lay such duties.

This is explicit about "pay all external taxes," and does not dance around the issue by dealing with duties to regulate commerce. (Franklin is consistent with his explicit statement of the previous year during his examination by the House of Commons: "An external tax is a duty laid on commodities imported.")

Benevolus discusses the situation from the viewpoint of a fellow Londoner.

> The distinction indeed between internal and external taxes is *here looked upon as groundless and frivolous*, and some are apt to

wonder how a sensible people should ever advance it. . . . However, whether there be validity in this distinction or not, seems to be immaterial; since *if they are willing to pay external though not internal taxes*, and we say they are the same, 'tis then the same thing to us, provided we get the same money from them, as much as they ought or are able to pay, and we may let them please themselves with their futile distinction as long as they think proper.[5]

In this April 14 letter to Joseph Galloway (a conservative leader in Philadelphia, and important friend to Franklin), Franklin explains his reason for such writing.

The Clamour has been, by Grenville's Party, with much Art and Industry, rais'd so high against America in general, that our Friends thought it not prudent to push [American affairs]. . . . I have written several Papers to abate a little if possible the Animosity stirr'd up against us, and flatter my self they may be attended with some Success. . . . They have been reprinted here in several of the Newspapers.

He adds this assessment of the ministry. "The Current [is] strong against America in general, which our Friends in the Ministry are oblig'd a little to give way to." He sees taxation on the horizon. "They have pledg'd themselves to Parliament for some Revenue to be rais'd from America. . . . I doubt People in Government here will never be satisfied without some Revenue from America, nor America ever satisfy'd with their imposing it."[6]

On May 2, Thomas Whately wrote John Temple. He disdains the internal/external distinction, and highlights what is now considered to be settled law.

The distinction between internal and external taxes frequently occurs, not now as a subject of debate, but a matter of reproach to those who maintain'd last year that Parliament had not a right to lay the former as well as the latter. I told you in my last that that doctrine was then always call'd nonsensical. It has been since said to be criminal and treasonable, & they who defended it then disclaim it now, by alleging that the *Declaratory Act has put an end to the question, & determin'd the law.*[7]

THE TOWNSHEND REVENUE ACT

Chancellor of the Exchequer Charles Townshend planned to raise money from America with duties imposed not for the regulation of trade, but imposed for the single purpose of revenue. On May 13, Townshend emphasized in the House of Commons that, although he was "clear in opinion that this country had a power of taxation of every sort, and in every case," he planned "to lay taxes upon America, but not internal taxes, because though he did not acknowledge the distinction, it was accepted by many Americans and this was sufficient."[8]

On May 16, Johnson wrote Pitkin to report Townshend's comments.

> Although he did not in the least doubt the right of Parliament to tax the Colonies internally, and that he knew no difference between internal and external taxes (which, by the way, is a doctrine very generally adopted here,) yet since the Americans were pleased to make that distinction, he was willing to indulge them, and chose for that reason to confine himself *to regulations of trade, by which a sufficient revenue might be raised in America.*[9]

The resulting Townshend Revenue Act (7 George III c. 46) was "An act for granting certain duties in the British colonies and plantations in America." The title continues about "more effectually preventing the clandestine running of goods in the said colonies and plantations," but provisions for doing so were separate from the levy of duties. The duties were imposed on a number of products "which shall be imported from Great Britain into any colony or plantation in America."[10] (In short: tea, paper, glass, and painter's colors.) The duties were collected at American ports, in the same manner as those of the Sugar Act, but there was no pretense they were for the regulation of trade; they were intended strictly to raise revenue. (Further raising the ire of Americans, the statute appropriated the revenue arising from payment of the duties to paying the salaries of British officials previously supported by colonial assemblies. Such a planned use for the revenue was, aside from the issue of taxation, a threat to the very existence of colonial legislatures.) The bill was quietly approved by both houses, and received the royal assent on June 29.[11]

The British, still believing Americans accepted external taxation even without the camouflage of trade regulation, were disconcerted when Americans interpreted those new duties as being unconstitutional. The colonies protested: petitions, nonimportation, violence. Resistance continued through all of 1768 and 1769. Of importance to our story, the violence involved not only resistance to the Townshend duties, but to regulations of the Sugar Act. Over and over again, violence, even rioting, was sparked by often-arbitrary decisions by customs officers to enforce provisions of the Sugar Act. A famous mob action (causing much distress in Britain) was the riot prompted by seizure of John Hancock's sloop *Liberty* in June 1768. The legal basis for the (perhaps unjustified) seizure varied over time but always for violation of Sugar Act regulations.[12]

AMERICA AWAKENS TO TAXATION

Reflection about the Townshend Revenue Act caused Americans to reconsider previous acts that dealt with exacting revenue from America through the use of duties collected at American ports.

Letters from a Farmer

American reaction to the Townshend duties was influenced by an extended essay published in the *Pennsylvania Chronicle* as a series of letters from early December 1767 to February 1768. They were written by sophisticated Philadelphia lawyer and politician John Dickinson. In order to adopt the persona of a simple farmer, he published them anonymously as *Letters from a Farmer in Pennsylvania, to the Inhabitants of the British Colonies* (known as the *Farmer's Letters*). The letters were said (by those who supported his ideas) to represent "a calm yet full inquiry into the right of the British parliament, lately assumed, to tax the American colonies; the unconstitutional nature of which attempt is maintained in a well-connected chain of close and manly reasoning."[13]

In letter two of December 7, 1767, he starts out by stating that the Townshend Revenue Act "appears to me to be unconstitutional," despite the fact that "parliament unquestionably possesses a legal authority to regulate the trade of Great Britain, and all her colonies."

> Here we may observe an authority expressly claimed and exerted to impose duties on these colonies; not for the regulation of trade . . . *but for the single purpose of levying money upon us.* This I call an innovation; and a most dangerous innovation.[14]

Duties for the regulation of trade are constitutional, while duties for the single purpose of revenue are not constitutional. This *trade-regulation criterion* avoids the distinction between internal and external taxes, substituting a determination of the purpose for which a duty is levied.

In letter four of December 21, Dickinson answers critics.

> An objection, I hear, has been made against my second letter, which I would willingly clear up before I proceed. "There is," say these objectors, "a material difference between the Stamp Act and the late act for laying a duty on paper, etc. [The objectors claim the] duties imposed by the Stamp Act were *internal* taxes; but the present are *external*, and therefore the parliament may have a right to impose them."

He responds. "To this I answer, with a total denial of the power of parliament to lay upon these colonies any 'tax' whatever." He continues. "Such persons therefore as speak of *internal* and *external* 'taxes,' I pray may pardon me, if I object to that expression, as applied to the privileges and interests of these colonies."[15]

Governor Bernard, in a letter of January 28, 1768, to Secretary at War Lord Barrington (Bernard's friend and mentor), set out his interpretation of the position taken by Dickinson.

> I understand that it is a prevailing Opinion on your side of the Ocean that America, if let alone will come to herself & return to the same Sense of Duty & obedience to Great Britain which she professed before. But It seems to me that observing & considerate Men on this side of the water expect no such thing.

He addresses port duties, and the external and internal tax issue.

Let us state the positions urged *in parliament on the behalf of the Americans* & the use which has been made of them in America, & see how far the chain of reasoning can be extended. It was said in parliament that

1. The parliament has no right to tax the Americans, because the Americans have no representatives in parliament.

2. But they have a right to impose *port duties or external taxes*, because such duties are for the regulation of trade.

Bernard asserts that friends of America in Parliament believe in the equivalence of external taxes and port duties for the regulation of trade

3. The difference between an external and an internal tax is that the former is imposed for the regulation of trade & the latter for raising a Revenue.

Then after a complex chain of reasoning, he characterizes the American position as stating that all port duties are internal taxes, saying that "the only Difference between the Port duties declared to be for raising a Revenue & those of which no such declaration is made is that in one the Intention is explicit; in the other it is implied." Bernard claims that he is presenting the American position.

This is not a fictitious Argument but a real one now urged & insisted upon as the terms of a good agreement between Great Britain & her Colonies. For proof of which I refer your Lordship to the *Farmer's Letters*, in which you will find the whole of this argument laid down either positively or consequentially.

He ends that, if Parliament takes "no notice of these American Pretensions," they will "become really, what they are now [proclaimed] to be, a Bill of American rights."[16]

Joseph Harrison, collector of customs for the port of Boston, while in the midst of a controversy over enforcement of Sugar Act regulations, provided insight into the mood of Americans when writing Lord Rockingham on June 17, 1768. Harrison explains how the *Farmer's Letters* were influencing American opinion. "A Series of Letters from a Farmer in Pensylvania to the Inhabitants of the British Colonies written by one Dickinson a Lawyer in Philadelphia . . . have been the principal means of spreading this almost general Disafection among the People."

> A dangerous and seditious combination has been formed to resist the execution of those Acts of Parliament . . . that impose any *Duties payable in the Colonies.* . . . A general Discontent begun to prevail and soon shewed itself by an almost universal Clamor against all Duties, Customs and Custom house Officers. *Even the penny a Gallon Duty on Molasses* [which] was admitted by the Americans themselves in 1766, as so proper and easy an Imposition, that no Objection could possibly be made to it is now found out to be oppressive and illegal: the common Cry being, Pay no Duties! [and] Save your Money and you save your Country![17]

Dickinson also drew attention from William Knox: *The Controversy Between Great Britain and Her Colonies Reviewed* (published in February 1769).[18] Knox ridicules without mercy the American stance as shifting from one argument to another.

> When the repeal of the stamp-act was their object, a distinction was set up between internal and external taxes; they pretended not to dispute the right of parliament to impose external taxes, or port duties . . . however productive of revenue they might be. . . . This, however, was only the language for 1765 and 1766, but when parliament seemed to adopt the distinction, and . . . imposed certain duties [on imports] . . . the distinction between internal and external taxes is rejected by the colony advocates, and a new one devised *between taxes for the regulation of trade, and taxes for the purpose of revenue.*

He derides and refutes the new distinction (making explicit reference to Dickinson), ending with, "This boasted *distinction* between taxes for the regulation of trade, and taxes for the purpose of revenue, *we therefore see is without a difference.*"[19]

All Other Acts of American Revenue Must Follow

On February 11, 1768, the Massachusetts assembly distributed an inflammatory circular letter that prompted extensive American protest to the Townshend duties. It subtly called for concerted action. "It seems to be necessary that all possible care should be taken that the representatives of the several assemblies, upon so delicate a point, should harmonize with each other."[20] Instead of continuing with the letter itself, it suits our story to instead look at a British perception of the letter: an interpretation sent to Secretary of State Shelburne by Governor Bernard on February 18.

> I now send your Lordship a Copy of this Circular Letter, which I would animadvert upon if the time would permit. At present I will only make two observations.

His first point is essentially that the Americans have changed the basis upon which they dispute the right of Parliament to levy taxes.

> 1. That this present undertaking is calculated to inflame the whole Continent, & engage them to join together in another Dispute with the Parliament, about the Authority of the latter; altho' *the present Subject Matter was professedly allowed by the Americans themselves* to be within the bounds of the power of Parliament at the time of the former dispute.

He next clarifies the vague "present Subject Matter" as meaning "duties [imposed] in the American Ports." Then he reaches the conclusion that the rationale for denial of authority to impose such duties is equally applicable to any statute enacted to gain revenue from America.

> 2. That the Distinctions, by means of which they now transfer the Matters contained in the late Act of Parliament from the range of *what they before conceded to Parliament* to that of what they before denied, is equally conclusive against all *Acts of Parliament imposing duties in the American Ports*, & consequently if the last Act should be given up to those pretensions, all other *acts of American revenue must follow*.[21]

Nonimportation

Although the American protests of 1768 and 1769 are not our story, there is one form of resistance that was soon to become important to the story of the Sugar Act. Governor Bernard explains the beginning of nonimportation in two March letters. He wrote Barrington on March 4, 1768, referring to a meeting of the Boston merchants earlier that day in which they propose nonimportation resolutions.

> The Traders here are now associating in the same Manner that they did at the Time of the Stamp Act; with what Success remains to be determined: however there is now a Subscription opened to import no British Goods (except for the Fishery) for 18 Months. If this was all, we Crown Officers should be very well Content: but it is given out among them that they will not submit to the Laws in the Mean Time; & violent methods of Opposition are every Day expected. One Man has unloaded a Cargo without entring it at the Custom House: it was done in the Night with a strong hand; but it is as publickly known as if it had been at Noon Day. The Officers either do not or dare not know where the Goods are carried.

Although starting at an eighteen-month boycott, the developing idea was to cease importation until the Townshend duties were repealed. Many Boston merchants were prepared to demand more.

> Many Merchants say they will not suffer Custom House Officers to go on board their Ships; one of them declared so in the House of Representatives. When they are asked what will satisfy them, the Answer is *a total Repeal of the Laws of Trade imposing Duties and nothing less.*

On the other hand, many merchants were hesitant about a boycott at all. On March 21, Bernard wrote Shelburne about the situation.

> This may be said to be the *first movement of the Merchants against the Acts of parliament*: all the proceedings before were carried on at town meetings, & were rather upon refinements of policy than concern for Trade. There never was less reason for the

Merchants to complain of the regulations of trade than at present [then giving reasons]. *However the Merchants are at length dragged into the Cause*; their intercourse & Connection with the politicians & the Fear of opposing the Stream of the people have at length *brought it about against the Sense of an undoubted Majority* both of members property & weight.

The development of agreements for nonimportation took many twists and turns, involving coordination with the merchants of New York and Philadelphia. But even as early as this spring of 1768, Bernard understood the intent of the merchants (and those pressuring the merchants to agree).

But it is scarce a Secret with any of them that the cheif intent of this Subscription is to raise an *alarm among the Merchants & Traders of Great Britain* & by means of popular discontent there to oblige the parliament to submit to their Terms in America. As this Game has been once before plaid with success [in 1765], it is no Wonder that they have great dependence upon it Now.

He could also see the ultimate goal.

In short, your Lordship may depend upon it that Nothing less than the *abolition of all Acts imposing Duties* is proposed. When that is done the transition to all other Acts of Parliament will be Very short & easy.[22]

Governor Bernard was prescient in seeing the upcoming American demand for *abolition of all acts imposing duties,* demands that wavered and twisted and changed, but that came to full fruition in 1774.

Nine

Demand for Repeal

"If the Americans found their petition upon that principle of right which goes agt raising any revenue at all in America, they ought to pray ... against all duties laid for revenue, [including] those very duties which a few years ago we were told they were so willing to pay."

—William Dowdeswell, August 1768

"You revived the scheme of taxation [and] then it was that they quarreled with the old taxes, as well as the new."

—Edmund Burke (to the House of Commons), April 1774

AMERICANS—THEIR ATTITUDE SHARPENED BY TAXES IMPOSED as port duties by the Townshend Revenue Act—finally came to protest the Sugar Act as taxation. Edmund Burke, in his April 19, 1774, *Speech on American taxation* in the House of Commons, explained how such protests came to pass.

When Parliament repealed the Stamp Act in the year 1766, I affirm, first, that the Americans did not, in consequence of this measure, call upon you to give up the former parliamentary revenue [i.e., the Sugar Act of 1764] which subsisted in that country; or even any one of the articles which compose it.

I affirm, also, that when, departing from the maxims of that repeal, you revived the scheme of taxation, and thereby filled the

minds of the Colonists with new jealousy, and all sorts of apprehensions, *then it was that they quarreled with the old taxes, as
well as the new*; then it was, and not till then, that they questioned
all the parts of your legislative power; and, by the battery of such
questions, have shaken the solid structure of this Empire to its
deepest foundations.[1]

The years 1768 and 1769 were filled with controversy and dissent,
petitions, associations to boycott British imports, and violence.
Americans dropped the distinction between internal and external
taxes, and objected to the old taxes as well as the new. The taxation
controversy waxed and waned for five more years, coming to a head
with the formation of the First Continental Congress in 1774.

THERE IS NO DISTINCTION

Parliamentary strategist William Dowdeswell, in a long political and
philosophical letter to Rockingham on August 14, 1768, addressed
American reaction to the Townshend Revenue Act. He is concerned
that other colonies might follow the example of Boston (the nonimportation association and the violent resistance in June to enforcement of the Sugar Act). He observes that the Townshend duties are
not "grievous burdens on the colonies," then brings out the real issue
and the necessary British response. "The people there [make their
stand] against the general principle of raising any revenue in America
& therefore extend their opposition even to a reduced duty on the
molasses." But for Parliament to repeal the act "would be avoiding
the real question."

> A repeated opposition . . . upon a principle directed against all
> duties for revenue must be met. It must either be admitted which
> is timidity, weakness, irresolution & inconsistency; or it must be
> resisted & ye [arms] of this Country must be exerted against her
> colonies.

He points out an inconsistency in the American protests.

> If the Americans found their petition upon that principle of right
> which goes agt raising any revenue at all in America, they ought

to pray not only [against the Townshend duties] but against all
duties laid for revenue, [including] *those very duties which a few
years ago we were told they were so willing to pay.*

Dowdeswell points out that "the distinction between external &
internal taxes has been found frivolous [by the Americans]. As indeed
I always thought it." He ends with the prediction that any British admission of the American claim of rights "will give them in my opinion a charter against being bound to any laws passed without their
consent."[2]

In the midst of a February 1769 debate in the House of Commons
"respecting the disturbances in America," Townshend's position toward taxation was defended; it "was not the opinion of one man,
but of numbers." And his imposition of taxes was all but obligatory.

He was anxious to impose taxes that would be acceptable to the
Americans; but in these hopes *he was misled by the Americans
themselves*; who said to him, "take the tax; let it but bear the *appearance of port duties*, and it will not be objected to." A Chancellor of the Exchequer at that time who had not attempted
something of the kind would have been looked upon as
blameable.[3]

A letter of early 1769 from the assembly of Massachusetts to
agent De Berdt makes it clear that American leaders see the connection between the Townshend duties, the Sugar Act, and the Stamp
Act—all explicit acts of taxation asserted by the Declaratory Act to
be within the authority of Parliament. There is no difference between
external and internal taxation; there is no distinction to be made.

When the Parliament, soon after the repeal of the stamp act,
thought proper to pass another act, declaring the authority, power,
and right of Parliament to make laws that should be binding on
the colonies, in all cases whatever, it is probable that acts for levying taxes on the colonies, *external and internal*, were included; for
the act made the last year, imposing duties on paper, glass, &c. *as
well as the sugar acts and the stamp act*, are, to all intents and
purposes, in form as well as in substance, as much revenue acts as

those for the land tax, customs and excises in England. The necessity of establishing a revenue in America is expressly mentioned in the preambles; they were originated in the honorable House of Commons, as all other money and revenue bills are; and the property of the colonies, with the same form, ceremony and expressions of loyalty and duty, is thereby given and granted to his Majesty, as they usually give and grant their own.[4]

OBSERVATIONS ON SEVERAL ACTS OF PARLIAMENT

Nonimportation, the American reaction having the most significance for the Sugar Act story, was slow to take effect, with considerable disagreement about the details of the boycott. But by the spring of 1769, merchants in Boston, Philadelphia, and New York had reached a degree of consensus, entering into separate associations for nonimportation, generally along the lines of continuing the boycott until the Townshend duties were repealed; but Boston merchants still rankled over the old taxes.

Later in the year, the association of Boston merchants began a turn toward more aggressive conditions for ending the boycott. On October 17, 1769, they revised their nonimportation agreement so as to demand that nonimportation should continue beyond repeal of the Townshend duties, and be contingent on the repeal of *all acts* imposing duties for raising a revenue in America—including those of the Sugar Act. On October 25, the merchants wrote their counterparts in Philadelphia, advocating they adopt the more aggressive policy. On November 11, the Philadelphia merchants responded to the Boston letter, agreeing only to the concept, not the action, but nonetheless explicitly condemning by name the revised Sugar Act.

The acts of the 4th and 6th George 3rd, being *expressly for the purpose of raising a revenue* and containing many grievous and unreasonable burdens upon trade [should be repealed, along with the Townshend Revenue Act].

The design of the Merchants through the continent was not only to procure a repeal of any Single Act but to give weight to the petitions [of their colonial legislatures] against the Parliament's claim to tax the Colonies; and to prevent any future attempts of like Nature; that a precedent admitted will operate against us; and that *an acquiescence under the acts of the 4th and 6th, even though that of the 7th of George 3d* [Townshend Revenue Act] *should be repealed, will be establishing a precedent.*

Despite that forceful statement, the Philadelphia merchants held back, claiming that since they had not earlier demanded repeal of the Sugar Act, "our Merchants are extremely averse to making it now an object of their non-importation agreement."[5] New York merchants declined a similar request to modify their nonimportation agreement. Lieutenant Governor Colden reported to Secretary of State Hillsborough on December 4. "Merchants of this Place received a Letter from the Massachusetts Bay, exhorting them to enter into new Resolutions of not importing any British Manufactures until all the acts of Parliament which lay duties on Goods Imported into the Colonies, are repealed. . . . Not one person spoke in favor of it."[6]

Given the refusal of the other merchants to take action, Boston merchants decided, for the sake of unanimity, not to insist upon the repeal of all duties. Although they agreed to resume importation when the Townshend duties were repealed, they still wanted to press for repeal of the Sugar Act. In this December 29 letter to Benjamin Franklin, they explain the situation regarding the status of the boycotts, and the failure to obtain wider agreement to their more aggressive approach. (A similar letter went to agent Dennys De Berdt.) They include this discussion about the Sugar Act.

As the Acts of the 4th and 6th George the third Contain many grievous and unreasonable restrictions upon Trade and are by far the most exceptionable, the Merchants here have tho't it necessary to make some Observations upon these Acts as also upon the Conduct of the Custom House Officers here that our Friends in Parliament may be acquainted with the Difficulties the Trade labors under by means of these Acts.[7]

The merchants enclosed their "Observations" in the form of a thirty-seven-page pamphlet: *Observations on Several Acts of Parliament, Passed in the 4th, 6th and 7th Years of His Present Majesty's Reign.*[8]

The representative body of this people having very fully and repeatedly remonstrated against these acts as unconstitutional and
as infringing the rights and privileges of the subject, it is unnecessary to add any thing upon that head; but we shall confine our
Remarks to such parts of these acts as affect the trading interest.

By these acts certain rates and duties are imposed on molasses,
sugars, wine, tea, glass, paper and many other articles commonly
imported into the British colonies in America. [Such] embarrassments on the trade of the colonies must greatly diminish if not
wholly destroy several branches of it.

The result, claim the merchants, would be to "lessen the demand
for British manufactures." The essay discusses the fishery at length,
repeating the rationale of the northern colonies in early 1764. The
molasses duty continues to be a burden.

[Several important] branches of trade are greatly obstructed by
the duties imposed, and the restrictions to which they are subjected by the aforementioned acts. *The duty on molasses, tho' reduced to one penny per gallon*, which at first sight may appear
but small, yet as it is one tenth part of the value (when brought to
market) is really large, and will be a discouragement to a trade
which has insinuated itself into, and is a great spring to every
branch of business among us. The fishery, the lumber trade and
ship-building, are greatly promoted by the importation of molasses, and distilling it into rum, and the trade to Africa wholly
depends on this article; so that any act which hath a tendency to
obstruct the importation of molasses must be prejudicial to Great-
Britain.

The revisions to the Sugar Act in 1766 changed the nature of the
molasses duty.

The former acts imposing duties on molasses were intended only
as a regulation of trade, and to encourage our own islands; and
the duty was only on foreign molasses. But by [the act of 1766] it
is imposed on all molasses, and *expressly for the purpose of raising a revenue.*

The high duty on foreign sugar "is a great burden on our trade to the foreign islands."

> If we confine ourselves to molasses, a sufficient return'd cargo *cannot always be obtain'd*; and the . . . duties upon sugars are so heavy as to render the import of them so unprofitable, that we cannot pursue a trade by which we disposed of the superfluous produce of our country.

Adding to the problems resulting from duties, the essay also addresses unreasonable regulations that placed additional burdens on American trade, "as mention'd in the act of the 6th of George the Third" (referring to restricting trade with northern Europe). After another twenty pages of grievances, the merchants return to molasses.

> When the duty upon molasses was sixpence sterling a gallon . . . it was well known in England the officers of the customs contrived at the importation, and their conduct was not disapproved. . . . *But since the duty on molasses has been reduced, the Whole, tho' grievous, has been regularly paid.*

At this point the merchants move beyond the topic stated in the title; many acts, even the Sugar Act of 1733, should be repealed.

> What the Colonists have a right to expect and hope for, is a repeal of all the acts imposing duties on any kind of goods imported into the British colonies for the purpose of raising a revenue in America, as being inconsistent with their rights as free subjects—the removal of every unnecessary burden upon trade, and that it be restor'd to the same footing it was upon before the act of the 6th of George the second, commonly call'd the sugar-act [i.e., the 1733 act]—particularly,
>
> That molasses, so necessary to promote every branch of trade, and likewise sugars, *be admitted free of duty.*

After more of the same, here is the central idea of the essay: restore trade to its status before 1733. Repeal of some duties "will not relieve the trade of the burdens it labours under."

But should all the revenue acts be repealed and the trade reliev'd from all unnecessary restrictions, and restor'd to the footing it was upon before the act of the 6th of George the second, and the indulgencies now mentioned be granted, it would have a happy tendency to unite Great-Britain and her colonies on a lasting foundation.

This is a call for repeal of the Townshend Revenue Act and all three Sugar Acts.

The embarrassments, difficulties and insupportable burdens under which this trade has laboured, have already made us prudent, frugal and industrious, and such a spirit in the Colonists must soon, very soon, enable them to subsist without the manufactures of Great-Britain, the trade of which, as well as its naval power, has been greatly promoted and strengthened by the luxury of the colonies; consequently any measures that have a tendency to injure, obstruct and diminish the American trade and navigation, must have the same effect upon that of Great-Britain, and, in all probability, PROVE HER RUIN.

Benjamin Franklin—and Dennys De Berdt as well—publicized the pamphlet, promoting its appearance in several influential magazines in London.[9]

THE RIGHT OF TAXING THE AMERICANS

On March 5, 1770, the House of Commons took up a debate on "a Motion to repeal the American Tea-Duty Bill [i.e., the Townshend Revenue Act]." Prime Minister Lord North was against repeal of the entire act. He moved to repeal all the duties of the act except that on tea, arguing it was necessary to keep the act in place in order to demonstrate *"the right of taxing the Americans."* The debate illustrates the continuing relevance of the Sugar Act.

Thomas Pownall moved to amend Lord North's proposal so as to also repeal the tea duty and hence the entire act. Pownall insisted that he was *not giving up the right of taxing the Americans.* Were it not for the Declaratory Act "and another, viz. 4th of Geo. 3 [the Sugar Act of 1764] exerting that right, I would not now take the part

I mean to take in this debate."[10] Lord North retorted that if Parliament yields to the new American distinction between duties based on their purpose (alluding to Dickinson's trade-regulation criterion), then "the Americans will call all duties for the purpose of a revenue; we shall call them for the purpose of trade. It is drawing a line which does not settle any one dispute." If Parliament were to repeal all the duties under pressure, then "*the next associations will be against the acts of the fourth and the sixth of the King. . . .* I go upon very good ground. In the course of the present year, many of the associations have declared that they will hold this language, *until all these revenue acts are repealed.* Therefore, Sir, upon my word if we are to run after America in search of reconciliation in this way, I do not know a single act of parliament that will remain." The debate went on, but Lord North had the votes: most duties were repealed, but the act and the duty on tea were retained.[11]

Many merchants having been hesitant about nonimportation in the first place, the limited repeal action brought about the results desired by British leaders. Although it was a complex, stumbling end to the coordinated boycott, the nonimportation movement soon collapsed.[12] A long period followed in which the Americans were mostly quiet about the laws of trade. The Sugar Act went on as before, with only intermittent complaint.

The calm was interrupted by the Tea Act in the spring of 1773. The resulting American agitation is not properly part of our story, but the tempest over tea stood in sharp contrast to continued American payment of the duties of the Sugar Act. One merchant argued that objecting to the tea duty was inconsistent with failure to protest the Sugar Act, writing this in the *Boston Evening Post* of October 25, 1773.

> What consistency is there in making a clamor about this small branch of the revenue [alluding to the tax on tea], whilst we silently pass over *the Articles of Sugar, Molasses, and Wine, from which more than three quarter parts of the American Revenue has and always will arise*, and when the Acts of Parliament imposing Duties on these Articles stand on the same Footing as that respecting Tea and the Moneys collected from them are applied to the same Purposes?[13]

Debate about an inconsistent American position persisted; a pamphlet published in 1774 by a prominent American loyalist makes the argument that the wine and molasses duties of the Sugar Act being accepted, the duties on tea ought to be accepted as well.

[We] have always allowed that [Parliament] had a right to regulate not only the trade, but all concerns of the Colonies; such a power they have always exercised, and we have submitted to their acts. *Thus, for instance, we have paid a duty on wine and molasses, in obedience to Parliament, and without protestations or remonstrances; and, for the same reasons we are as much obliged to pay the duty on tea.* If we would act consistently, we should either refuse to pay the duty on wine and molasses, or consent to pay it on tea; for it is, in both cases, imposed from the same principle, and has the same effect.[14]

The rest of the story is well known: the Boston Tea Party in December 1773 resulted in punitive action by Parliament in 1774, which resulted in American agitation, culminating in a congress of the colonies.

FIRST CONTINENTAL CONGRESS

In the First Continental Congress, Americans made a unified statement regarding the Sugar Act; they called for—they demanded—its repeal. On October 14, 1774, the congress stated rights and grievances. The preamble starts with this assertion, exactly on point to the Sugar Act.

Whereas, since the close of the last war, the British parliament, claiming a power of right to bind the people of America by statutes in all cases whatsoever, hath, in some acts expressly imposed taxes on them, and in others, *under various pretences, but in fact for the purpose of raising a revenue*, hath imposed rates and duties payable in these colonies.

That preamble is followed by rights stated as resolves.

The inhabitants of the English colonies in North-America, by the immutable laws of nature, the principles of the English constitution, and the several charters or compacts, have the following rights:

This resolve deals with the authority of Parliament, the central issue in the constitutional conflict.

Resolved, 4. That the foundation of English liberty, and of all free government, is a right in the people to participate in their legislative council: and as the English colonists are not represented, and . . .

The final portion of the resolve is directly relevant to trade regulation, and to the Sugar Act.

But, from the necessity of the case, and a regard to the mutual interest of both countries, *we cheerfully consent* to the operation of such acts of the British parliament, as are bona fide, restrained to the *regulation of our external commerce*, for the purpose of securing the commercial advantages of the whole empire to the mother country, and the commercial benefits of its respective members; *excluding every idea of taxation, internal or external*, for raising a revenue on the subjects in America, without their consent.[15]

This statement thoroughly rejects any parliamentary control of internal commerce, and places adherence to parliamentary regulation as being based on American consent. An earlier proposition (by the conservative James Duane) suggested that "we cheerfully acknowledge that it belongs only to Parliament to direct & superintend the Trade of all his Majesty's Dominions."[16]

It was John Adams who wrote the final version of the resolution, and was the advocate for the assertive phrases regarding *consent* and limiting parliamentary regulation to *external commerce*. On December 12, Adams wrote a delegate from Pennsylvania asking about acceptance of his resolution.

Let me know how the fourth resolution in our bill of rights is relished and digested among the choice spirits along the continent. I had more anxiety about that, than all the rest. But I find it is extremely popular here. Our provincial Congress have approved and adopted it in strong terms. They consider it as a great point gained. They think it has *placed our connection with Great Britain on its true principles*, and that there is no danger from it to us, and there is quite as much allowed to her as either justice or policy requires.[17]

At the end of the statement of ten "indubitable rights and liberties," the congress moved to grievances. "In the course of our inquiry, we find many infringements and violations of the foregoing rights, which, from an ardent desire that harmony and mutual intercourse of affection and interest may be restored, we pass over for the present, and proceed to state *such acts and measures as have been adopted since the last war*, which demonstrate a system formed to enslave America."[18]

The following unnumbered resolve demands repeal of the Sugar Act, naming the acts of 1764 and 1766.

Resolved. The following acts of parliament are infringements and violations of the rights of the colonists; and that *the repeal of them is essentially necessary, in order to restore harmony between Great Britain and the American colonies*, viz.:

The several acts of 4 Geo. 3. ch. 15 . . . 6 Geo. 3. ch. 52 . . . which impose duties for the purpose of raising a revenue in America . . . are subversive of American rights.[19]

As a final note on the importance of the Sugar Act, here is a list of duties specified in the Continental Association—the hammer behind the demands of the Continental Congress, a "non-importation, non-consumption, and non-exportation agreement." The core of the agreement is this. "We do solemnly bind ourselves and our constituents, under the ties aforesaid, to adhere to this association, until such parts of the several acts of parliament passed since the close of the last war, as impose or continue duties on tea, wine, molasses, syrups, paneles, coffee, sugar . . . are repealed."[20]

NOTES

PREFACE

1. Edmund Burke, *Speech of Edmund Burke, Esq. on American Taxation, April 19, 1774* (London: J. Dodsley, 1775), in Paul Langford, ed., *The Writings and Speeches of Edmund Burke, Party, Parliament, and the American Crisis 1766-1774*, vol. 2 (Oxford, UK: Clarendon Press, 1981), 408-63 (quotations, 428, 434). Hereafter, [Burke], *Speech on American Taxation*.

2. Worthington Chauncey Ford, ed., *Journals of the Continental Congress, 1774-1789*, vol. 1, *1774* (Washington: Government Printing Office, 1904), 71.

INTRODUCTION

1. Joseph J. Ellis, *The Cause: The American Revolution and Its Discontents, 1773-1783* (New York: Liveright, 2021), 7.

2. Charles Francis Adams, ed., *The Works of John Adams, Second President of the United States*, vol. 10 (Boston: Little, Brown, 1856), 345. To William Tudor, August 11, 1818.

3. Ford, ed., *Journals of the Continental Congress*, 1:71.

4. Commentary in Randolph G. Adams, *Political Ideas of the American Revolution*, 3rd ed. (New York: Barnes & Noble, 1958. First edition 1922), 19. In a more colorful phrase, "Taxation was to be the anvil on which the Anglo-American relationship broke." Peter D. G. Thomas, *Revolution in America: Britain and the Colonies, 1763–1776* (Cardiff: University of Wales Press, 1992), 15. On the other hand, other issues cannot be ignored. The Sugar Act "contained a number of requirements that simply made colonial trade more complicated, more difficult, and therefore more costly and less profitable. It was objectionable not only because it was a tax." John McCusker and Russell Menard, *The Economy of British America, 1607-1786* (Chapel Hill: University of North Carolina Press, 1985), 356. Historian Bernard Bailyn offers an additional view. When introducing "evidence that a design against liberty was unfolding," he starts with "the invasion of customs officers . . . reinforced by the new tax measures [including] the Sugar Act of 1764." Bernard Bailyn, *The Ideological Origins of the American Revolution* (Cambridge, MA: Harvard University Press, 2017, originally published 1967), 102-05.

PROLOGUE

1. Molasses is a byproduct of the production of sugar from sugarcane. If it can be sold (to be used as an inexpensive sweetener or for distillation into rum) rather than discarded, it can be a small but significant component affecting the

profitability of a sugar plantation, alternatively allowing the sale of sugar at a lower price.

2. Cecil Headlam and Arthur Percival Newton, eds., *Calendar of State Papers: Colonial Series, America and West Indies,* vol. 37, *1730* (London: His Majesty's Stationery Office, 1937), 303.

3. *Cobbett's Parliamentary History of England, from the Norman Conquest, in 1066, to the Year 1803, AD 1722–1733,* vol. 8 (London: Printed by T. C. Hansard, 1811), 856-57. I have added italics to these and to other quotations throughout the book.

4. Adam Anderson and William Coombe, *Anderson's Historical and Chronological Deduction of the Origin of Commerce, From The Earliest Accounts: Containing An History Of The Great Commercial Interests Of The British Empire,* vol. 3 (Dublin: Printed by P. Byrne, 1790), 433.

5. *The Political State of Great Britain. Containing The Months of July, August, September, October, November, and December. 1731,* vol. 42 (London: Printed for the Executors of Mr. Boyer, 1731), 639.

6. Anderson and Coombe, *Historical and Chronological Deduction,* 3:433-34. "Legally limiting North America's commerce with the . . . foreign sugar growers in the West Indies would diminish their ability to compete in Europe." John Mc-Cusker and Russell Menard, *The Economy of British America, 1607-1786* (Chapel Hill: University of North Carolina Press, 1985), 163.

7. *The British Empire in America, consider'd, in a second letter, from a gentleman of Barbadoes, to his friend in London* (London, 1731), 10.

8. Cecil Headlam and Arthur Percival Newton, eds., *Calendar of State Papers: Colonial Series, America and West Indies,* vol. 39, *1732* (London: His Majesty's Stationery Office, 1939), 45.

9. John Russell Bartlett, ed., *Records of the Colony of Rhode Island and Providence Plantations, in New England: 1757-1769,* vol. 6 (Providence: By Order of the General Assembly, 1861), 421.

10. *Cobbett's Parliamentary History of England,* 8:996-98. A detailed discussion of the complex situation is provided by: Dorothy Burne Goebel, "The 'New England Trade' and the French West Indies, 1763-1774: A Study in Trade Policies," *WMQ,* vol. 20, no. 3 (July 1963), 331-372.

11. Gertrude S. Kimball, ed., *The Correspondence of the Colonial Governors of Rhode Island 1723-1775,* vol. 1 (New York: Houghton, Mifflin, 1902), 25, 26.

CHAPTER 1: THE SUGAR ACT OF 1733

1. "The object of this law was not to raise a revenue, but to hamper the development of the French colonies, and to prevent the importation of their produce into the English possessions. Hence the duties were made so high as to be virtually prohibitive." George Louis Beer, *British Colonial Policy, 1754-1765* (New York: Macmillan, 1907), 22.

2. "The most notable general feature of the year was the continuing interest taken by each House of Parliament in colonial affairs. . . . Much time had been devoted to the debates on the Sugar Bill, and the petitions presented by those

who supported and those who opposed it had excited much attention." Cecil Headlam and Arthur Percival Newton, eds., *Calendar of State Papers: Colonial Series, America and West Indies,* vol. 40, *1733* (London: His Majesty's Stationery Office, 1939), v.

3. *Cobbett's Parliamentary History of England,* 8:1197-99.

4. Kimball, ed., *Correspondence of the Colonial Governors of Rhode Island,* 1:34.

5. *Cobbett's Parliamentary History of England,* 8:1262-63, 1266.

6. Headlam and Newton, eds., *Calendar of State Papers:1733,* 40:66. The New York petition requested that the "Province may be exempted from the Sugar Bill, or that they may be heard against it etc., since it 'will be very prejudicial to the Trade and Navigation, and tend greatly to the impoverishment of H.M. faithfull subjects in the Northern Colonies, particularly in the said Province.'" Ibid., 67. The editors of the *Calendar of State Papers* make this comment. "The petition goes far beyond the economic question as to the advisability of the proposed duty. It raises in unmistakable words the constitutional plea of 'No taxation without representation,' which was to play such an outstanding part in the controversies preceding the American Revolution, and it is therefore worthy of note that more than thirty years before the Stamp Act the argument should be so conclusively stated." Ibid., xxxiii.

7. Danby Pickering, *The Statutes at Large, from the Second to the 9th year of King George II,* vol. 16 (Cambridge, UK: Printed by Joseph Bentham, 1765), 374-379. All 1733 Sugar Act quotations are from this source.

8. [C. F.] Adams, ed., *Works,* 10:346. To William Tudor, August 16, 1818.

9. The situation surrounding the issue of admiralty courts is complex. For an extended discussion, see Carl Ubbelohde, *The Vice-Admiralty Courts and the American Revolution* (Chapel Hill: University of North Carolina Press, 1960), particularly chapter 2.

10. Merrill Jensen, ed., *American Colonial Documents to 1776,* English Historical Documents, vol. 9 (London: Eyre & Spottiswoode, 1955), 374.

11. "Plead the general issue" means a plea that denies a complaint in its entirety without admitting the truth of any allegations.

12. In contemporary writing, the act was referred to as the Sugar Act. In modern discourse it is commonly known as the Molasses Act. For additional background, see Albert B. Southwick, "The Molasses Act—Source of Precedents," *William and Mary Quarterly* 8, no. 3 (1951): 389-405; Richard B. Sheridan, "The Molasses Act and the Market Strategy of the British Sugar Planters," *Journal of Economic History* 17, no. 1 (1957): 62-83; and Ken Shumate, "The Molasses Act: A Brief History," *Journal of the American Revolution: Annual Volume 2020* (Yardley, PA: Westholme Publishing, 2020), 8-20.

13. Headlam and Newton, eds., *Calendar of State Papers, 1733,* 40:169.

14. McCusker and Menard, *Economy of British America,* 144-45.

15. [Burke], *Speech on American Taxation,* 427.

16. John Lind, *Remarks on the Principal Acts of the Thirteenth Parliament of Great Britain* (London: Printed for T. Payne, 1775), 1:219. Lind was a paid pamphleteer and persistent critic of the American position on colonial rights.

17. Frank Wesley Pitman, *The Development of the British West Indies, 1700-1763* (New Haven, CT: Yale University Press, 1917), 281.
18. Jack P. Greene, ed., *Great Britain and the American Colonies, 1606-1763* (Columbia: University of South Carolina Press, 1970), 290-92.
19. *The Fitch Papers, Volume II: January 1759-May 1766*, Collections of the Connecticut Historical Society, vol. 18 (Hartford, CT: The Society, 1920), 77.

CHAPTER 2: REVISE AND ENFORCE
1. What the British perceived as a lack of support from the colonies during the Seven Years' War, the "inconstancy of the American colonists," led to the need for a change in colonial policy, "a complete overhaul of the colonial system." Thomas C. Barrow, *Trade and Empire: The British Customs Service in Colonial America, 1660-1775* (Cambridge, MA: Harvard University Press, 1967), 173. In fact, "The difficulty in securing adequate support from the colonies during the war with France . . . convinced the British government that *parliamentary taxation* was the sole and only means of obtaining from the colonies their just share of the cost of their own defence." However, taxation was not the only unprecedented aspect to the act. It was expected "to reform the old colonial system, both in its administrative and in its economic features. . . . [It] marked a radically new departure in colonial policy." Beer, *British Colonial Policy*, 269-70, 277.
2. Ford, ed., *Journals of the Continental Congress*, 1:91; L. H. Butterfield, ed., *The Adams Papers, Diary and Autobiography of John Adams*, vol. 2, *1771–1781* (Cambridge, MA: Harvard University Press, 1961), 76. As a consequence, this moment was the beginning of the end to "widespread general satisfaction with the system as it existed prior to 1764." The resulting revision to the Sugar Act of 1733 implemented a change of policy "where the dominant motive was not regulation and development, but regulation for the sake of revenue and political exploitation." It was "a revolution in the century-old trade and navigation system." Oliver M. Dickerson, *The Navigation Acts and the American Revolution* (Philadelphia: University of Pennsylvania Press, 1951), xiii, xiv.
3. "The sequence of events leading directly to the American Revolution commenced with the ministry headed by George Grenville between 1763 and 1765." P. D. G. Thomas, "George III and the American Revolution," *History* 70, no. 228 (1985): 16-31 (quotation, 18). For detail on the fateful decisions leading up to this point, see Thomas C. Barrow, "Background to the Grenville Program, 1757-1763," *WMQ* 22, no. 1 (1965): 93-104.
4. Charles M. Andrews, *England's Commercial and Colonial Policy, The Colonial Period of American History*, vol. 4 (New Haven, CT: Yale University Press, 1964, first published 1938), 218.
5. Danby Pickering, *The Statutes at Large, from Magna Charta to the end of the Eleventh Parliament of Great Britain, Anno 1761*, vol. 25 (Cambridge, UK: Printed by Joseph Bentham, 1763), 345, 347-48. A side effect of the use of the Royal Navy led to problems in America. "The Hovering Act . . . resulted in the empowering of naval officers stationed on ships off the North American and West Indian coasts to act in suppressing illegal trade." The problem was that

"the new officers of enforcement lacked a nice understanding of what, for the sake of efficiency and national advantage, should be ignored and what enforced in the navigation laws." Alfred S. Martin, "The King's Customs: Philadelphia, 1763-1774." *WMQ* 5, no. 2 (1948): 201-16 (quotation, 204-05).

6. John L. Bullion, *A Great and Necessary Measure: George Grenville and the Genesis of the Stamp Act* (Columbia: University of Missouri Press, 1982), 78-79, 103; Barrow, *Trade and Empire*, 177.

7. James Munro, ed., *Acts of the Privy Council of England: Colonial Series, AD 1745-1766*, vol. 4 (London, 1911), 569.

8. According to historian Merrill Jensen, except for the large illicit trade with foreign colonies in the West Indies, "the great bulk of American trade flowed in the legal channels established by the Acts of Trade and Navigation. Nevertheless, customs officials and naval officers in America seemed to spend more time using the technicalities of the laws to harass legal traders than in search for smugglers." Merrill Jensen, *The Founding of a Nation: A History of the American Revolution, 1763-1775* (New York: Oxford University Press, 1968), 330. There is evidence to support the contention of low levels of illicit trade with Europe. "Although the exact extent of smuggling cannot be determined with accuracy because of the nature of the smugglers' activities, we can establish its limits. We know that great quantities of European goods . . . passed through England as the law required. In comparison with the volume of such trade, the amount of goods smuggled was necessarily small because by far the greater percentage of colonial shipping is known to have been engaged in legal trades, and, however illicit their intentions, the smugglers could not find sufficient cargo capacity to present formidable competition." Lawrence A. Harper, "The Effect of the Navigation Acts on the Thirteen Colonies," published in Richard B. Morris, ed., *The Era of the American Revolution* (New York: Columbia University Press, 1939), 3-39 (quotation, 4). It is worth noting that the analysis by Harper overlooks that shipping of foreign nations and their trading companies might provide cargo capacity for illicit trade. Overall, the evidence either for or against the amount of illicit trade with Europe is sparse. "The nature of the smuggling that went on during our colonial period is very simple, though the extent of it and the relation of it to the total volume of colonial trade is very difficult to determine. It is doubtful if satisfactory conclusions can ever be reached on these points owing both to the lack of evidence and to its unsatisfactory character." Charles M. Andrews, "Colonial Commerce," *American Historical Review* 20, no. 1 (1914): 43–63 (quotation, 61). In the end however, what British leaders *believed to be true* was the defining factor in development of the Sugar Act.

9. Bullion, *Great and Necessary Measure*, 84-86.

10. Ninetta S. Jucker, ed., *The Jenkinson Papers, 1760-1766* (London: Macmillan, 1949), 254. Wood was a highly respected, long-serving subminister, considered expert on American revenue matters.

11. The report is presented and discussed in George Bancroft, *History of the United States, from the discovery of the American continent*, vol. 5 (Boston: Little, Brown, 1875), 88-89n, and Jensen, *Founding of a Nation*, 71.

12. Colin Nicolson, ed., *The Papers of Francis Bernard: Governor of Colonial Massachusetts, 1760-1769, Volume 1: 1759-1763,* The Colonial Society of Massachusetts, vol. 73 (Boston: Colonial Society of Massachusetts, 2007), 390.

13. John W. Tyler and Elizabeth Dubrulle, eds., *The Correspondence of Thomas Hutchinson, Volume 1: 1740-1766.* The Colonial Society of Massachusetts, vol. 84 (Boston: Colonial Society of Massachusetts, 2014), 179.

14. Nicolson, ed., *Papers of Francis Bernard,* 73:401.

15. Nicolson, ed., *Papers of Francis Bernard,* 73:381-82. The editor of the Bernard papers comments that, "This is the first official notification that [Francis Bernard] and the other governors received of Britain's intention to reinvigorate the mercantilist system by improving both enforcement of the trade laws and revenue collection. The ensuing controversy is traditionally regarded as the onset of the imperial crisis that presaged the Revolution."

16. Frederick W. Ricord and Wm. Nelson, eds., *Documents Relating to the Colonial History of the State of New Jersey 1757-1767,* First ser., vol. 9 (Newark, NJ: Daily Advertiser Printing House, 1885), 98.

17. *Jasper Mauduit: Agent in London for the Province of the Massachusetts-Bay 1762–1765,* Massachusetts Historical Society Collections, vol. 74 (Boston: The Society, 1918), 130, 131.

18. Leonard W. Labaree, ed., *The Papers of Benjamin Franklin,* vol. 10 (New Haven, CT: Yale University Press, 1966), 415.

19. William Nelson, ed., *New Jersey Archives: Newspaper Abstracts, vol. 5: 1762-1765* (Paterson, NJ: Call Printing and Publishing, 1902), 203.

20. Colin Nicolson, ed., *The Papers of Francis Bernard: Governor of Colonial Massachusetts, 1760–1769, Volume 2: 1764–1765,* The Colonial Society of Massachusetts, vol. 81 (Boston: Colonial Society of Massachusetts, 2012), 29.

21. Leonard W. Labaree, ed., *The Papers of Benjamin Franklin,* vol. 11 (New Haven, CT: Yale University Press, 1967), 215.

CHAPTER 3: REASONS AGAINST THE RENEWAL

1. *Journals of the House of Representatives of Massachusetts: 1763-1764,* vol. 40 (Boston: Massachusetts Historical Society, 1970), 132. The following text from the memorial is abstracted from Charles M. Andrews, "State of the Trade, 1763," *Publications of the Colonial Society of Massachusetts: Transactions, 1916-1917,* vol. 19 (Boston, 1918), 379-90.

2. "This last contention was not true, as events later proved, but for the present the merchants persuaded the various New England legislatures to adopt their arguments and support their cause." Jack M. Sosin, *Agents and Merchants: British Colonial Policy and the Origins of the American Revolution, 1763-1775* (Lincoln: University of Nebraska Press, 1965), 43n.

3. As abhorrent as was the slavery in the West Indies, the slave trade and treatment of slaves must be addressed as an integral part of eighteenth-century commerce. "Slavery is of course fundamental to the history of the eighteenth-century West Indies." The islands' wealth was based on, "the ruthless exploitation of a labour force of some half a million enslaved Africans and their constant replenishment by new imports." P. J. Marshall, *Edmund Burke and the British Empire*

in the West Indies: Wealth, Power, and Slavery (Oxford, UK: Oxford University Press, 2019), 2.

4. Andrews, "State of the Trade, 1763," 19:379-81. Despite the assurances of the merchants (and later independent action of the assembly), Massachusetts never made an official protest against the renewal of the act of 1733.

5. *Reasons against the renewal of the Sugar Act as it will be prejudicial to the trade, not only of the northern colonies, but to that of Great-Britain also.* (Boston: Province of the Massachusetts-Bay, 1764). For more background on the development and use of the pamphlet, and on the essays and petitions discussed in this chapter, see Ken Shumate, "Reasons against the Renewal of the Sugar Act," *JAR*, June 4, 11, and 18, 2020.

6. *An Essay on the Trade of the Northern Colonies of Great Britain in North America*, in Merrill Jensen, ed., *Tracts of the American Revolution, 1763-1776* (Indianapolis, IN: Bobbs-Merrill, 1966), 3-18.

7. Bartlett, ed., *Records of the Colony of Rhode Island*, 6:378-83.

8. Lawrence Henry Gipson, *Jared Ingersoll: a Study of American Loyalism in Relation to British Colonial Government* (New Haven, CT: Yale University Press, 1920), 113; *Fitch Papers*, 18:277-79.

9. Charles M. Andrews, "The Boston Merchants and the Non-importation Movement," *Publications of the Colonial Society of Massachusetts: Transactions, 1916-1917*, vol. 19 (Boston, 1918), 159-259 (quotation, 166n).

10. *Journal of the Votes and Proceedings of the General Assembly of the Colony of New-York*, vol. 2 (New York: Published by Order of the General Assembly, 1766), 740-44.

11. Bernard Knollenberg, *Origin of the American Revolution: 1759–1766* (New York: Macmillan, 1960), 148.

12. Robert J. Taylor, "Israel Mauduit," *New England Quarterly* 24, no. 2 (1951): 208-30.

13. "The vigorous protests of the New England merchants" against renewal of the act of 1733, "do not contain a single word that can be construed as a denial of the legality of the act itself." The Rhode Island remonstrance (for example) declared the act to be highly injurious and detrimental, "but not once did they say that parliament had no legal right to pass such a measure." Charles M. Andrews, *The Colonial Background of the American Revolution: Four Essays in American Colonial History* (New Haven, CT: Yale University Press, 1924), 62.

14. Thomas Whately, *The Regulations Lately Made Concerning the Colonies, and the Taxes Imposed Upon Them, Considered* (London: Printed for J. Wilkie, 1765), in Gordon S. Wood, ed., *The American Revolution: Writings from the Pamphlet Debate 1764–1776*, vol. 1 (New York: Library of America, 2015), 165-240 (quotation, 234). Hereafter [Whately], *Regulations Lately Made*.

15. Lind, *Remarks on the Principal Acts*, 1:223.

16. James Otis, *The Rights of the British Colonies Asserted and Proved* (Boston, 1764) in Bernard Bailyn, ed., *Pamphlets of the American Revolution, 1750–1776: vol. 1, 1750-1765* (Cambridge, MA: Harvard University Press, 1965), 418-82 (quotation, 467-68). Hereafter, [Otis], *Rights of the British Colonies Asserted and Proved*.

17. Richard Price, *Observations on the Nature of Civil Liberty, the Principles of Government, and the Justice and Policy of the War with America* (London: Printed for T. Cadell, 1776), 25.

18. *Jasper Mauduit: Agent in London,* 74:145-46.

19. Bernard Bailyn, ed., *Pamphlets of the American Revolution, 1750–1776:* vol. 1, 1750-1765 (Cambridge, MA: Harvard University Press, 1965), 358-59. He includes among the statements of colonial opinion yet another essay against renewal, the anonymous 1764 *Considerations Upon the Act of Parliament Whereby a Duty is laid of six Pence Sterling per Gallon on Molasses.* Historian Gordon Wood has pointed out that "the colonists had more or less avoided confronting the constitutionality of the Molasses Act by smuggling and bribery." Gordon S. Wood, *Power and Liberty: Constitutionalism in the American Revolution* (New York: Oxford University Press, 2021), 11.

CHAPTER 4: THE SUGAR ACT OF 1764

1. [Burke], *Speech on American Taxation,* 428, 430.

2. Ford, ed., *Journals of the Continental Congress,* 1:76.

3. Sir Lewis Namier & John Brooke, *The House of Commons, 1754-1790,* vol. 2 (London: Her Majesty's Stationary Office, 1964), 145.

4. *The Parliamentary History of England, From the Earliest Period to the Year 1803,* vol. 15. A. D. 1753-1765 (London: Printed by T.C. Hansard, 1813), 1337, 1340-41.

5. R. C. Simmons and P. D. G. Thomas, eds., *Proceedings and Debates of the British Parliaments Respecting North America, 1754-1783,* vol. 1, *1754-1764* (Millwood, NY: Kraus International, 1982), 486.

6. Peter D. G. Thomas, *British Politics and the Stamp Act Crisis: The First Phase of the American Revolution, 1763-1767* (Oxford, UK: Clarendon Press, 1975), 52-53.

7. The following account is based on P. D. G. Thomas, ed., "Parliamentary Diaries of Nathaniel Ryder. 1764–7," *Camden Miscellany* vol. 23, Camden Society, 4th ser., vol. 7 (London: Royal Historical Society, 1969), 234-38. Hereafter, Ryder, *Diaries.*

8. The controversy over stamp duties is well documented. See Edmund S. Morgan & Helen M. Morgan, *The Stamp Act Crisis: Prologue to Revolution* (Chapel Hill: University of North Carolina Press, 1953), and Thomas, *British Politics and the Stamp Act Crisis.* The main feature of the Stamp Act of 1765, and the American grievance, was that it interfered with the internal polity of the colonies by requiring many legal documents (and other paper items such as newspapers) to be on taxed paper sold by those appointed as *stamp distributors.* It was considered to be an "inland tax," an "internal tax."

9. Reports of the discussion on this topic give varied reasons for the postponement, "and the subsequent misrepresentation of them reveal something of the confusion, misunderstanding, and duplicity which plagued Anglo-American relations in the period leading up to the Revolution." Edmund S. Morgan, "The Postponement of the Stamp Act," *WMQ* 7, no. 3 (1950): 353-92 (quotation, 355).

10. The following account is based on Simmons and Thomas, eds., *Proceedings and Debates,* 1:492-95.

11. *Parliamentary History of England,* 15:1434. For further background about the Sugar Act, see Allen S. Johnson, "The Passage of the Sugar Act," *WMQ* 16, no. 4 (1959): 507-14, and Ken Shumate, "The Sugar Act: A Brief History," *JAR,* September 17, 2018.

12. [Whately], *Regulations Lately Made.* See also, Ian R. Christie, "A Vision of Empire: Thomas Whately and the Regulations Lately Made concerning the Colonies," *English Historical Review* 113, no. 451 (1998): 300-320.

13. [Whately], *Regulations Lately Made,* 167, 203-05, 222-23.

14. Danby Pickering, *The Statutes at Large, from Magna Charta to the end of the Eleventh Parliament of Great Britain, Anno 1761,* vol. 26 (Cambridge, UK: Printed by Joseph Bentham, 1764), 33-52. All 1764 Sugar Act quotations are from this source. My discussion of the text of the Sugar Act includes both block quotes and inline quotes. Unless indicated otherwise, all quotes are from the text of the Sugar Act as given in *Statutes at Large.*

15. [Whately], *Regulations Lately Made,* 222.

16. The duties and regulations regarding French wines changed over time; importation was often prohibited.

17. They also address pimento, but I largely ignore it, as well as other products that have little effect on the overall story of the Sugar Act.

18. [Whately], *Regulations Lately Made,* 215.

19. Ibid., 218-21.

20. Lind, *Remarks on the Principal Acts,* 1:259.

21. [Whately], *Regulations Lately Made,* 214.

22. Ford, ed., *Journals of the Continental Congress,* 1:84. The wine issue is complex. "It is probable that the new wine duties had a more serious effect upon the total course of colonial trade than did the much more widely discussed changes in the duty on molasses." Dickerson, *Navigation Acts,* 177. Historian Arthur Schlesinger, asserting that the effect of the wine duty was so pervasive that "one might add in supplementation of John Adams' remark concerning molasses that *wine was another essential ingredient* of American independence." Arthur M. Schlesinger, *The Colonial Merchants and the American Revolution, 1763-1766* (New York: Columbia University, 1918), 98.

23. [Whately], *Regulations Lately Made,* 217.

24. The reading is not easy. "It is a challenge to the reader's attention and patience to follow these provisions; but a comprehension of them *is essential to an understanding* of the attitude of colonial merchants and shipowners . . . *throughout the remaining years of the pre-Revolutionary period.*" Bernhard Knollenberg, *Growth of the American Revolution: 1766-1775* (Indianapolis, IN: Liberty Fund, 2003, originally published 1975), 21. Mindful of the challenge to the reader's attention, I do not address every section or every regulation.

25. [Whately], *Regulations Lately Made,* 228. Such naturalization was a lucrative business. "In some islands fully half of the sugar certified as British was of French origin. Some estates exported sugar without producing any at all. Mo-

lasses, rum, and sugar were [all] naturalized in the same way." Dickerson, *Navigation Acts,*188. Dickerson uses this regulation as an example of a broader issue. "It has been customary to blame the Sugar Act to the greed of the West India sugar planters, especially those resident in England and with seats in the House of Commons. That they supported the bill is certain, but an analysis of the bill fails to show that they received unusual benefits from the act." Ibid., 174.

26. [Whately], *Regulations Lately Made,* 228.

27. Ibid.

28. Ibid.

29. Oxenbridge Thacher, *The Sentiments of a British American* (Boston: Edes & Gill, 1764) in Bailyn, ed., *Pamphlets,* 1:490-98 (quotation, 494). Hereafter [Thacher], *Sentiments of a British American.*

30. [Whately], *Regulations Lately Made,* 227.

31. Ibid., 228.

32. Labaree, ed., *Papers of Benjamin Franklin,* 11:235.

33. Pickering, *Statutes at Large,* 26:430-44 (quotation, 440).

34. [Whately], *Regulations Lately Made,* 228-29.

35. "This section, together with the bonding provisions, made the law incapable of literal compliance in many parts of America." For the most part, knowledgeable customs officials recognized the problem. "The universal practice at most ports in America was to load and then furnish the various bonds, certificates, and other papers necessary for a proper clearance." And away from the ports themselves, it was "the usual practice for customs officers to cooperate with the trade in adjusting local practices to local conditions." Dickerson, *Navigation Acts,*181, 237, 220.

36. [Whately], *Regulations Lately Made,* 229.

37. William Allen and Lewis Burd Walker, *Extracts from Chief Justice William Allen's Letter Book* (Pottsville, PA: Standard Publishing, 1897), 65.

38. *The Bowdoin and Temple Papers,* Massachusetts Historical Society, 6th ser., vol. 9 (Boston: The Society, 1897), 53. To John Temple.

39. I have been characterizing the "Sugar Act" as being comprised of the three major acts of 1733, 1764, and 1766 (the acts most protested by the Americans). That is a useful simplification, but at this point it is worth noting that, in a broader sense, the modifications made by 5 George III c. 45 (including further clarification and restriction) are part of the Sugar Act. In fact, the title of the act includes the phrase, "An act for more effectually *securing and encouraging the trade* of his Majesty's American dominions." There being other related acts, the "Sugar Act" could be thought of as a wide-ranging group of parliamentary actions.

40. Pickering, *Statutes at Large,* 26:442.

41. *Observations on a Late State of the Nation* (London: J. Dodsley, 1769), in Langford, ed., *Writings and Speeches of Edmund Burke,* 2:102-219 (quotation, 182).

42. [Whately], *Regulations Lately Made,* 230.

43. Ibid.

44. The changes are complex. See Ubbelohde, *Vice-Admiralty Courts*, 48-54.

45. Ford, ed., *Journals of the Continental Congress*, 1:85, 91.

46. [Thacher], *Sentiments of a British American*, 493.

47. Colin Nicolson, ed., *The Papers of Francis Bernard: Governor of Colonial Massachusetts, 1760-1769, Volume 3: 1766-1767*, Publications of the Colonial Society of Massachusetts, vol. 83 (Boston: Colonial Society of Massachusetts, 2013), 144. The problem was not easy to solve. "The Customs Commissioners in England finally sent instructions to the colonial collectors to inform all of the [Royal Navy] sea captains that they were to report immediately to the custom-houses every time they seized a vessel." Such directions were easier to issue than to enforce. "The naval officers, eager enough to make seizures, were not pleased with the prospect of losing part of their profits by consulting with customs officers." Ubbelohde, *Vice-Admiralty Courts*, 78.

48. Pickering, *Statutes at Large*, 26:443.

49. Ubbelohde, *Vice-Admiralty Courts*, 50-51.

50. Knollenberg, *Origin of the American Revolution*, 179. Knollenberg characterizes sections 43 and 46 as "encouraging reckless seizures and suits of alleged violations of acts of trade and customs." Ibid., 357.

51. [Thacher], *Sentiments of a British American*, 494-95.

52. [Whately], *Regulations Lately Made*, 224-27.

53. Jucker, ed., *Jenkinson Papers*, 348. Jenkinson to Wolters. Here is a modern, less sanguine point of view about submitting to the evil. "The Sugar Act of 1764 was clearly a major successor to the great navigation act of the late seventeenth century . . . designed to tighten the navigation system." The consequence of stringent new regulations to accomplish its goal was that "so many more American shippers were required to post bonds and obtain certificates of clearance that nearly all colonial merchants, even those involved only in the coastwise trade, found themselves enmeshed in a bureaucratic web of bonds, certificates, and regulations." Gordon S. Wood, *The American Revolution: A History* (New York: Modern Library, 2002), 23.

54. [Burke], *Speech on American Taxation*, 429.

55. [Whately], *Regulations Lately Made*, 231.

56. Ford, ed., *Journals of the Continental Congress*, 1:71-72. I have reformatted (for readability) objections stated by the First Continental Congress in 1774.

57. Danby Pickering, *The Statutes at Large, from Magna Charta to the end of the Eleventh Parliament of Great Britain, Anno 1761*, vol. 26 (Cambridge, UK: Printed by Joseph Bentham, 1764), 103-05.

58. Ford, ed., *Journals of the Continental Congress*, 1:71.

59. Todd Andrlik, *Reporting the Revolutionary War: Before it was History, it was News* (Naperville, IL: Sourcebooks, 2012), 4.

60. *Jasper Mauduit: Agent in London*, 74:147n.

61. Ryder, *Diaries*, 302.

62. *The Examination of Doctor Benjamin Franklin, before an August Assembly*, in Wood, ed., *American Revolution: Writings*, 1:335-61 (quotations, 339-40, 341, 343, 348, 359).

63. Bailyn, *Ideological Origins*, 212-13.

64. [Burke], *Speech on American Taxation*, 2:430, 434.

65. Bailyn, *Pamphlets*, 1:356.

CHAPTER 5: PROTEST

1. Wood, *Power and Liberty,* 11.

2. According to Lawyer-Historian John Phillip Reid, "There was perhaps no error more egregious than the frequent assumption by British officials that when American whigs objected to internal taxation they were saying that taxes not internal—external taxes whatever they might be—were constitutional. The error led to a *misunderstanding that devolved into a belief* that external taxes were constitutionally acceptable to the colonists." John Phillip Reid, *The Authority to Tax*, vol. 2 of *Constitutional History of the American Revolution* (Madison: University of Wisconsin Press, 1987), 33.

3. I deal at length with the protests in *1764: The First Year of the American Revolution* (Yardley, PA: Westholme Publishing, 2021).

4. *Journal of the Votes and Proceedings of the General Assembly of the Colony of New-York,* 779.

5. Connecticut General Assembly, *The Public Records of the Colony of Connecticut [1636-1776],* vol. 9 (Hartford, CT: Press of the Case, 1890), 653-71 (quotations, 661, 670).

6. Labaree, ed., *Papers of Benjamin Franklin,* 11:76.

7. *A Report of the Record Commissioners of the City of Boston, Containing the Boston Town Records, 1758 to 1769* (Boston, 1886), in Merrill Jensen, ed., *American Colonial Documents to 1776,* English Historical Documents, vol. 9 (London: Eyre & Spottiswoode, 1955), 663-64.

8. *Journals of the House of Representatives of Massachusetts: 1764-1765,* vol. 41 (Boston: Massachusetts Historical Society, 1971), 76-77.

9. Thomas Hutchinson, *Strictures upon the Declaration of the Congress at Philadelphia: In a Letter to a Noble Lord, &c* (London, 1776), in Wood, ed., *American Revolution: Writings,* 1:775-800 (quotation, 777).

10. Massachusetts, *Proceedings of the Massachusetts Historical Society,* vol. 13 (Boston: Massachusetts Historical Society, 1875), 190.

11. Nicolson, ed., *Papers of Francis Bernard,* 81:90.

12. Massachusetts, *Proceedings of the Massachusetts Historical Society,* vol. 20 (Boston: Massachusetts Historical Society, 1884), 51.

13. Alden Bradford, ed., *Speeches of the Governors of Massachusetts from 1765 to 1775* (Boston: Printed by Russell and Gardner, 1818), 21-23.

14. Labaree, ed., *Papers of Benjamin Franklin,* 11:350-51.

15. Bartlett, ed., *Records of the Colony of Rhode Island,* 6:415.

16. "With such a universal denial of Parliament's right to tax, it is surprising that the protests against the Sugar Act did not emphasize the question of right more than they did. Most colonies chose to regard it as a regulation of trade, which it was, rather than a revenue measure, which it also was." Morgan & Morgan, *Stamp Act Crisis,* 40. John Phillip Reid also addressed the nature of colonial protests. He contends that the Sugar Act "was not protested as quickly

as the Stamp Act because it was not as obviously a tax measure. The Sugar Act was susceptible to various readings." The colonists often "described the Sugar Act not as a tax regulating trade but as a 'prohibition' on trade." Reid, *Authority to Tax*, 2:202.

17. Franklin B. Dexter, ed., *"A Selection from The Correspondence and Miscellaneous Papers of Jared Ingersoll,"* Papers of the New Haven Colony Historical Society, vol. 9 (New Haven, CT: The Society, 1918), 201-472 (quotation, 297).

18. *Bowdoin and Temple Papers*, 24-25.

19. *Letters from a Farmer in Pennsylvania, to the Inhabitants of the British Colonies* (Philadelphia: Printed by David Hall, 1768), in Paul Leicester Ford, ed., *The Writings of John Dickinson*, vol.1 *Political Writings: 1764-1774* (Philadelphia: Historical Society of Pennsylvania, 1895), 345n (quotation from letter 6, January 4, 1768). Hereafter [Dickinson], *Letters from a Farmer*. Edmund Morgan had this to say. "The Stamp Act appeared to most colonists to be the more dangerous, but in formulating their ideas of Parliamentary power they could not afford to neglect either measure; they had to decide in what way their rights were affected both by the internal taxes of the Stamp Act and by the external taxes of the Sugar Act." Edmund S. Morgan, "Colonial Ideas of Parliamentary Power 1764-1766," *WMQ* 5, no. 3 (1948): 311-41 (quotation, 313).

20. Lind, *Remarks on the Principal Acts*, 1:256-57, 271.

21. *Bowdoin and Temple Papers*, 43.

22. Great Britain. Parliament. House of Commons. *Journals of the House of Commons*, vol. 30 (London: H.M. Stationery Off., 1803), 90.

23. Ryder, *Diaries*, 254, 256-57. By internal duty Beckford was referring to stamp duties; by external duty he was referring to customs duties, "taxing the imports and exports."

24. *Bowdoin and Temple Papers*, 49.

25. *Fitch Papers*, 18:319.

26. In addition to universal protest as formal legislative action by the colonies, American protests involved effective nonimportation of British goods, a boycott that prompted British merchants and manufacturers to petition Parliament for repeal of the act. Most effective of all was violence and threats of violence against stamp distributors, halting the issuance of stamps and essentially nullifying the Stamp Act.

27. John Phillip Reid has addressed the absence of constitutional protests in 1765 regarding the Sugar Act, ending with the Stamp Act Congress. "Perhaps the most persuasive illustrations are provided by the Stamp Act Congress." His specific example is that although admiralty courts were protested on constitutional grounds, not so regarding duties. The "objections to the Sugar Act were commercial, not legal, complaining that it was 'burthensome' on trade, not that it was an unconstitutional tax. That pattern of argument was even more pronounced in the petitions the congress submitted." Although constitutional objections to the Stamp Act were clear, "when the revenue aspects of the Sugar Act were considered, the constitutional expressions disappeared and the grievance was stated entirely in economic terms." Reid, *Authority to Tax*, 2:201. Edmund

Morgan has expressed a different opinion. "The Stamp Act Congress . . . produced a set of resolutions and three petitions, to the King, the Lords, and the Commons, all denying the authority of Parliament to tax the colonies. Here as in the other formal colonial statements of this year there is no distinction made between internal and external taxes. . . . Though it acknowledged due subordination to Parliament, it denied without qualification the right of Parliament to tax the colonies." Morgan, "Colonial Ideas," 324-25. Substantial additional discussion is provided in Morgan & Morgan, *Stamp Act Crisis*, Chapter 7, especially the "Note on Internal and External Taxes," 119-21.

28. John Adams, William Tudor, and Daniel Leonard, *Novanglus, And Massachusettensis; Or, Political Essays, Published in the Years 1774 And 1775* (Boston: Hews & Goss, 1819), 173.

29. Ibid., 100.

30. [Burke], *Speech on American Taxation*, 434-35.

CHAPTER 6: THE BRITISH RETREAT

1. The Stamp Act was repealed on March 18, 1766, not as an admission that it violated the rights of the colonists, not as a surrender to the violent American resistance, but rather as an act that was inexpedient at the time and was "attended with many inconveniences." It was accompanied by a Declaratory Act that reaffirmed the authority of Parliament over the colonies, particularly asserting full power and authority to pass statutes with "sufficient force and validity to bind the colonies and people of America, subjects of the crown of Great Britain, *in all cases whatsoever.*"

2. William James Smith, ed., *The Grenville papers: being the correspondence of Richard Grenville, earl Temple, K.G., and the right Hon: George Grenville, their friends and contemporaries*, vol. 3 (London: John Murray, 1853), 215-16.

3. Paul Langford, *The First Rockingham Administration: 1765-1766* (London: Oxford University Press, 1973), 4.

4. R. C. Simmons and P. D. G. Thomas, eds., *Proceedings and Debates of the British Parliaments Respecting North America, 1754-1783*, vol. 2, *1765-1768* (Millwood, NY: Kraus International, 1983), 192. Historian Paul Langford explained that the ministry "emphasized again and again during the examination of witnesses in the House of Commons, that the Opposition's prophecies would be proved wrong." And further, "During the examination of [merchant] witnesses in Committee, discussion of the effects of the stamp tax constantly gave way to digressions on the trading situation in general." For some important discussions, "the Stamp Act problem was positively a distraction from the strictly commercial issues." Langford, *First Rockingham Administration*, 195, 199.

5. "The campaign of the British merchants and manufacturers for repeal of the Stamp Act was merely an interlude in their program of 'commercial reform' which began before the Stamp Act became an issue in British politics and which continued after its repeal." Specifically, "the 'American' merchants in Britain supported the complaints of the mainland merchants and demanded repeal of the strict trade regulations of the Grenville ministry and of the duties on foreign molasses." Jensen, *Founding of a Nation*, 174, 176.

6. Lucy S. Sutherland, "Edmund Burke and the First Rockingham Ministry," *EHR* 47, no. 185 (1932):46–72 (quotation, 62n).

7. Edmund S. Morgan, *Prologue to Revolution: Sources and Documents on the Stamp Act Crisis, 1764-1766* (Chapel Hill: University of North Carolina Press, 1959), 129.

8. Albert Matthews, ed., *Letters of Dennys De Berdt 1757-1770* (Cambridge, MA: Wilson and Son, 1911), 308.

9. Great Britain, *Journals of the House of Commons*, 30:462.

10. George Thomas Keppel, Earl of Albemarle, ed., *Memoirs of the Marquis of Rockingham and his contemporaries: With original letters and documents now first published*, vol. 1 (London: Richard Bentley, 1852), 304-06.

11. Andrew Stephen Walmsley, *Thomas Hutchinson and the Origins of the American Revolution* (New York: New York University Press, 1999), 75.

12. *Commerce of Rhode Island, [1726-1800]*, Collections of the Massachusetts Historical Society, Seventh ser.—vol. 9 (Boston: The Society, 1914), 140, 143.

13. Great Britain, *Journals of the House of Commons*, 30:598.

14. Leonard W. Labaree, ed., *The Papers of Benjamin Franklin*, vol. 13 (New Haven, CT: Yale University Press, 1969), 177-79.

15. "London Merchants on the Stamp Act Repeal," *Proceedings of the Massachusetts Historical Society*, Third ser., vol. 55 (Boston: The Society, 1923), 215-23 (quotation, 216-17).

16. *Commerce of Rhode Island*, 145, 146.

17. Thomas W. Copeland, ed., *The Correspondence of Edmund Burke*, vol. 1 (Cambridge, UK: The University Press, 1958), 239-240. To Charles O'Hara, a member of the Irish Parliament.

18. Matthews, ed., *Letters of Dennys De Berdt*, 314, 315.

19. Danby Pickering, *The Statutes at Large, from Magna Charta to the end of the Eleventh Parliament of Great Britain, Anno 1761*, vol. 27 (Cambridge, UK: Printed by John Archdeacon, 1767), 19-20.

20. Keppel, ed., *Memoirs of the Marquis of Rockingham*, 1:287.

21. "In drawing up the Declaratory Act, [Rockingham] deliberately phrased it in such a way as to leave the meaning uncertain to those whom it might offend. The result was that the colonists at first misunderstood Parliament's declaration of right." Morgan & Morgan, *Stamp Act Crisis*, 287.

22. James Truslow Adams, *Revolutionary New England, 1691-1776* (Boston: Atlantic Monthly Press, 1923), 341.

23. "London Merchants on the Stamp Act Repeal," 219.

24. Smith, *Grenville Papers*, 3:237-38. An editorial explanation adds that the comment was handwritten on the letter by a British official, Mr. Thomas Astle.

25. Nicolson, ed., *Papers of Francis Bernard*, 83:135.

26. Harry Alonzo Cushing, ed., *The Writings of Samuel Adams, 1764-1769*, vol. 1 (New York: G. P. Putnam's Sons, 1904), 387-88. A political essay of October 2, 1769.

27. Ford, ed., *Journals of the Continental Congress*, 1:92.

28. Smith, ed., *Grenville papers*, 3:250. To Mr. Nugent.

29. William Knox, *The Present State of the Nation: Particularly with Respect to its Trade, Finances, etc. etc. Addressed To The King And Both Houses Of Parliament* (Dublin: Printed for W. Watson, 1768), 26, 27, 29.

CHAPTER 7: THE SUGAR ACT OF 1766

1. The phrase "Sugar Act of 1766" is convenient for our purposes but is not common. In contemporary use, the act was rarely referred to by itself, rather described in tandem with the act of 1764 in a manner such as "the acts of the 4th and 6th George the third." Any singular reference to *Sugar Act* after 1766 implicitly referred to the act of 1764 as modified by the act of 1766 (as well as the rarely mentioned act of 1765).
2. Adams, *Revolutionary New England*, 340n.
3. John Fortescue, ed., *The Correspondence of King George the Third from 1760 to December 1783*, vol. 1 (London: Macmillan, 1927), 282.
4. Simmons and Thomas, eds., *Proceedings and debates*, 2:360.
5. Copeland, ed., *Correspondence of Edmund Burke*, 1:252. To Charles O'Hara.
6. Simmons and Thomas, eds., *Proceedings and debates*, 2:376-78.
7. Sutherland, "Edmund Burke," 71.
8. Great Britain, *Journals of the House of Commons*, 30:811.
9. Sutherland, "Edmund Burke," 50, 66-67, 69n.
10. Bartlett, ed., *Records of the Colony of Rhode Island*, 6:491.
11. Great Britain, *Journals of the House of Commons*, 30:813.
12. The act is 6 George III c. 49. Like the Sugar Act, it provides funds to support British forces in America. Monies from duties in excess of expenses for execution of the act "shall be paid into the receipt of his Majesty's exchequer . . . towards defraying the necessary expences of defending, protecting, and securing, the British colonies and plantations in America." Pickering, *Statutes at Large*, 27:266.
13. Pickering, *Statutes at Large*, 27:275-87. All 1766 Sugar Act quotations are from this source.
14. Ford, ed., *Journals of the Continental Congress*, 1:92.
15. Economist Adam Smith, writing in 1776, advanced this rationale for the geographic limitation. "The parts of Europe which lie south of Cape Finisterre [i.e., southern Europe], are not manufacturing countries, and we were less jealous of the colony ships carrying home from them any manufactures which could interfere with our own." Adam Smith, *An Inquiry into the Nature and Causes of the Wealth of Nations*, vol. 2 (London: Printed for W. Strahan and T. Cadell, fifth edition, 1789; first edition 1776), 175-76, in Edwin Cannan, ed., [Adam Smith] *The Wealth of Nations, with an introduction and notes* (London: Methuen, 1904), 546.
16. Pickering, *Statutes at Large*, 27:303-04.
17. Merrill D. Peterson, comp., *Thomas Jefferson: Writings* (New York: Library of America, 1984), 108-09.
18. Great Britain, *Journals of the House of Commons*, 30:845.
19. Samuel Eliot Morison, ed., *Sources & Documents Illustrating the American*

Revolution: 1764-1788, Second Edition (London: Oxford University Press, 1965. Published by the Clarendon Press, 1929), 74, 78-79.

20. "Officers harassing small vessels in coastwise trade could justify themselves by the printed instructions." The instructions did not provide "any indication of an exception to be made in favor of small coasting vessels, decked or undecked, with respect to the bonds required." Knollenberg, *Growth of the American Revolution*, 357, note 50.

21. Nicolson, ed., *Papers of Francis Bernard*, 83:164.

22. "London Merchants on the Stamp Act Repeal," 220-22.

23. Mary Bateson, ed., *A Narrative of the Changes in the Ministry 1765-1767* (London: Longmans, Green, 1898), 79. Described by the Duke of Newcastle in a letter of July 11, 1766.

24. Langford, ed., *Writings and Speeches of Edmund Burke*, 2:55.

25. Thomas Hutchinson, *The History of the Province of Massachusetts Bay: from 1749 to 1774*, vol. 3 (London: John Murray, 1828), 164.

26. John Almon, *A collection of interesting, authentic papers: relative to the dispute between Great Britain and America: showing the causes and progress of that misunderstanding, from 1764 to 1775* (London: Printed for J. Almon, 1777), 163-67.

27. Thomas Pownall, *The Administration of the British Colonies*, fifth edition, vol. 1 (London: Printed for J. Walter, 1774), 255.

28. Andrews, "The Boston Merchants and the Non-importation Movement," 174.

29. Nicolson, ed., *Papers of Francis Bernard*, 83:279-80.

30. W. S. Taylor and J. H. Pringle, eds., *Correspondence of William Pitt, Earl of Chatham*, vol. 3 (London: John Murray, 1839), 186, 188-89.

31. Matthews, ed., *Letters of Dennys De Berdt*, 451.

32. "If the colonists had been more intent on their theoretical rights than on immediate business concessions, the keener minds would have perceived that rejoicing was premature." It was a tax. "It was an unvarnished contradiction of the colonial claim to 'no taxation without representation.'" Schlesinger, *Colonial Merchants*, 85.

33. "The Act produced more revenue in the colonies than any other Act ever passed by Parliament." Jensen, ed., *American Colonial Documents*, 9:696. Although much more revenue was raised from the colonies by taxes collected in Great Britain (for example that on tobacco) and by the overall effect of the Navigation Acts, it was these visible taxes collected in the colonies that were the fundamental driver of American discontent.

34. This table is adapted from Table-25-2, in Alvin Rabushka, *Taxation in Colonial America* (Princeton, NJ: Princeton University Press, 2008), 753. The extant data regarding duties collected is sparse and inconsistent between various contemporary sources; but although the exact figures are uncertain, the overall picture is clear.

35. The additional revenue from seizures was small, a total of £10,000 for the years 1768 to 1774. Seizures by ships-of-war were almost 60 percent, the re-

mainder by customs officers. Edward Channing, *The American Revolution, 1761-1789*, A History of the United States, vol. 3 (New York: Macmillan, 1912), 89n.

36. Dickerson, *Navigation Acts*, 185, especially Table 9. Channing's data for molasses duties in 1773 and 1774 support the Dickerson results, with an even higher proportion of revenue from the molasses tax. In addition, Channing's figures demonstrate that the uproar over the 1773 tea legislation did not disturb the continued payment of duties for molasses. He shows molasses duties paid in 1773 of almost £15,000, and an increase in 1774 to over £17,000. In contrast, duties paid on tea dropped by over 75 percent. Channing, *American Revolution*, 3:90-91.

37. Dickerson, *Navigation Acts*, 187.

38. For elaboration, see Ken Shumate, "The Exception to 'no taxation without representation,'" *JAR*, September 9, 2019.

CHAPTER 8: A DISTINCTION WITHOUT A DIFFERENCE

1. There is a school of thought that argues the British were on the wrong road. We saw (chapter 5) Edmund Morgan make the case that the Americans never suggested that external taxation was acceptable, and saw John Phillip Reid assert that the British understanding was a misunderstanding.

2. "The Trumbull Papers," *Collections of the Massachusetts Historical Society*, 5th ser., vol. 9 (Boston: The Society, 1885), 243, 215-16.

3. Ryder, *Diaries*, 331; *Bowdoin and Temple Papers*, 79-80.

4. Sir Lewis Namier and John Brooke, *Charles Townshend* (London: Macmillan, 1964), 186-87.

5. Leonard W. Labaree, ed., *The Papers of Benjamin Franklin*, vol. 14 (New Haven, CT: Yale University Press, 1970), 114-15.

6. Ibid., 124, 125.

7. *Bowdoin and Temple Papers*, 83.

8. Ryder, *Diaries*, 344.

9. "The Trumbull Papers," 9:229.

10. Pickering, *Statutes at Large*, 27:503-512 (quotations, 503).

11. "Never could a fateful measure have had a more quiet passage." There was good reason for such concord. "Within the context of the British understanding of the imperial relationship there was no ground of political or constitutional argument on which any opposition to the Townshend duties could have been based. . . . There is no evidence of any opposition to or even criticism of the Townshend duties by colonial agents at the time of their enactment." Thomas, *Townshend Duties Crisis*, 32, 33.

12. D. H. Watson, "Joseph Harrison and the Liberty Incident," *WMQ* 20, no. 4 (1963): 585-95.

13. [Dickinson], *Letters from a Farmer*, 279-80. The praise is an editorial comment about the letters, quoting the *London Monthly Review* as representing "the English Whig view."

14. Ibid., 312, 316.

15. Ibid., 328, 332.

16. Colin Nicolson, ed., *The Papers of Francis Bernard: Governor of Colonial Massachusetts, 1760-1769, Volume 4: 1768*, Publications of the Colonial Society of Massachusetts, vol. 86 (Boston: Colonial Society of Massachusetts, 2015), 81-83.

17. Watson, "Joseph Harrison and the Liberty Incident," 588.

18. William Knox, *The Controversy Between Great Britain and Her Colonies Reviewed* (London: printed for J. Almon, 1769), in Wood, ed., *American Revolution: Writings*, 1:615-66.

19. Ibid., 631, 635.

20. Bradford, ed., *Speeches of the Governors*, 134.

21. Nicolson, ed., *Papers of Francis Bernard*, 86:98-99.

22. Ibid., 135-38.

CHAPTER 9: DEMAND FOR REPEAL

1. [Burke], *Speech on American Taxation*, 411.

2. Warren M. Elofson, *The Rockingham Connection and the Second Founding of the Whig Party 1768-1773* (Montreal: McGill-Queens's University Press, 1996), 43.

3. Sir Henry Cavendish, *Debates of the House of commons, during the thirteenth Parliament of Great Britain, commonly called the unreported Parliament*, vol. 1 (London: Longman, Orme, Brown, & Green, 1841), 213. The defense was offered in a debate of February 8, 1769, Townshend having died in September 1767.

4. Bradford, ed., *Speeches of the Governors*, 125. Letter of January 12, 1769.

5. Schlesinger, *Colonial Merchants*, 131-33.

6. *The Colden Letter Books vol. 2. 1765–1775*, Collections of the New York Historical Society, vol. 10 (New York: Printed for the Society, 1877), 193.

7. William B. Willcox, ed., *The Papers of Benjamin Franklin*, vol. 16 (New Haven, CT: Yale University Press, 1972), 272-73.

8. *Observations on several acts of Parliament, passed in the 4th, 6th and 7th years of His present Majesty's reign: and also, on the conduct of the officers of the customs, since those acts were passed, and the Board of Commissioners appointed to reside in America. Published by the merchants of Boston* (Boston: Printed by Edes & Gill, 1769). All quotations from the pamphlet are from this source. "This pamphlet was the clearest and strongest statement ever formulated of the position of the American merchant class, particularly that of New England." Schlesinger, *Colonial Merchants*, 133. The pamphlet "summed up the whig constitutional position." John Philip Reid, *The Authority to Legislate*, Constitutional History of the American Revolution, vol. 3 (Madison: University of Wisconsin Press, 1991), 219.

9. For a longer elaboration of the place of the pamphlet in American protests, see Ken Shumate, "Observations on Several Acts of Parliament," *JAR*, June 9, 2021.

10. *The Parliamentary History of England, From the Earliest Period to the Year 1803*, vol. 16. A. D. 1765-1771 (London: Printed by T.C. Hansard, 1813), 851, 854, 857.

11. Cavendish, *Debates of the House of commons*, 1:487. The partial repeal (10 George III c. 17) received the royal assent on April 12, 1770, to be effective in December.

12. The partial repeal, intended "as a gesture to placate the colonists," was effective. "Most colonial merchants, frightened by mob violence and the political aspirations of the popular classes at home, rested content with the redress of their immediate economic grievances after 1770." McCusker and Menard, *Economy of British America*, 356.

13. Jane Kamensky, *A Revolution in Color: The World of John Singleton Copley* (New York: W. W. Norton, 2016), 203.

14. Thomas Bradbury Chandler, *A Friendly Address to all Reasonable Americans on the Subject of our Political Confusions; in which the Necessary Consequences of violently opposing the King's Troops, and of a General Non-importation are Fairly Stated* (America [New York]: Printed [by James Rivington] for the purchasers, 1774), in Wood, ed., *American Revolution: Writings*, 2:271-314 (quotation, 276).

15. Ford, ed., *Journals of the Continental Congress*, 1:63, 67, 68-69. John Phillip Reid maintains that this resolution "was a prime condition for remaining under British rule, for it resolved the only outstanding constitutional question concerning the authority of Parliament to regulate imperial trade." John Phillip Reid, *Constitutional History of the American Revolution*, Abridged Edition (Madison: University of Wisconsin Press, 1995), 77. On the other hand, Gordon Wood has stated that this approach by the congress to "allow Parliament to have power over their external commerce," and phrasing ("necessity of the case, and a regard to the mutual interest of both countries") to be "awkwardly put" and "not a very satisfactory solution to the problem." Wood, *Power and Liberty*, 28.

16. Paul Hubert Smith ed., *Letters of Delegates to Congress, 1774-1789*, vol. 1, *August 1774-August 1775* (Washington: Library of Congress, 1976), 41. "The main difference between this acknowledgment and those of the 'conservatives' such as Duane, is that Parliament's jurisdiction was limited to 'our external commerce.' In the future the imperial legislature would not have jurisdiction over intercolonial or intracolonial trade." Reid, *Authority to Legislate*, 3:242-43.

17. Charles Francis Adams, ed., *The Works of John Adams, Second President of the United States*, vol. 9 (Boston: Little, Brown, 1854), 350. Adams to Edward Biddle.

18. What the colonies shared in common could be told as "a single story that pivoted on 1763." The start of the story was defined by the Continental Congress. "The decision to focus on British policy after 1763 was made after lengthy debates in closed session of the Rights and Grievances Committee." Ellis, *The Cause*, 38, 333 (note 55).

19. Ford, ed., *Journals of the Continental Congress*, 1:71.

20. Ibid., 76, 79-80. The agreement was made on October 20.

BIBLIOGRAPHY

Adams, Charles Francis, ed. *The Works of John Adams, Second President of the United States,* vol. 9. Boston: Little, Brown, 1854.

———. *The Works of John Adams, Second President of the United States,* vol. 10. Boston: Little, Brown, 1856.

Adams, James Truslow. *Revolutionary New England, 1691-1776.* Boston: Atlantic Monthly Press, 1923.

Adams, John, William Tudor, and Daniel Leonard. *Novanglus, And Massachusettensis; Or, Political Essays, Published in the Years 1774 And 1775.* Boston: Hews & Goss, 1819.

Adams, Randolph G. *Political Ideas of the American Revolution,* 3rd ed. New York: Barnes & Noble, 1958. First edition 1922.

Allen, William and Lewis Burd Walker. *Extracts from Chief Justice William Allen's Letter Book.* Pottsville, PA: Standard Publishing, 1897.

Almon, John. *A collection of interesting, authentic papers: relative to the dispute between Great Britain and America: showing the causes and progress of that misunderstanding, from 1764 to 1775.* London: Printed for J. Almon, 1777.

Anderson, Adam and William Coombe. *Anderson's Historical and Chronological Deduction of the Origin of Commerce, From The Earliest Accounts: Containing An History Of The Great Commercial Interests Of The British Empire,* vol. 3. Dublin: Printed by P. Byrne, 1790.

Andrews, Charles M. "Colonial Commerce," *American Historical Review* 20, no. 1. 1914.

———. "State of the Trade, 1763," *Publications of the Colonial Society of Massachusetts: Transactions, 1916-1917,* vol. 19. Boston, 1918.

——. "The Boston Merchants and the Non-importation Movement," *Publications of the Colonial Society of Massachusetts:
Transactions, 1916-1917,* vol. 19. Boston: 1918.

——. *The Colonial Background of the American Revolution: Four
Essays in American Colonial History.* New Haven, CT: Yale University Press, 1924.

——. *England's Commercial and Colonial Policy, The Colonial Period of American History,* vol. 4. New Haven, CT: Yale University
Press, 1964, first published 1938.

Andrlik, Todd. *Reporting the Revolutionary War: Before it was History, it was News.* Naperville, IL: Sourcebooks, 2012.

Bailyn, Bernard, ed. *Pamphlets of the American Revolution, 1750–
1776:* vol. 1, *1750-1765.* Cambridge, MA: Harvard University
Press, 1965.

Bailyn, Bernard. *The Ideological Origins of the American Revolution.* Cambridge, MA: Harvard University Press, 2017, originally
published 1967.

Bancroft, George. *History of the United States, from the discovery
of the American continent,* vol. 5. Boston: Little, Brown, 1875.

Barrow, Thomas C. "Background to the Grenville Program, 1757-
1763," *William and Mary Quarterly* 22, no. 1. 1965.

——. *Trade and Empire: The British Customs Service in Colonial America, 1660-1775.* Cambridge, MA: Harvard University Press, 1967.

Bartlett, John Russell, ed. *Records of the Colony of Rhode Island
and Providence Plantations, in New England: 1757-1769,* vol. 6.
Providence: By Order of the General Assembly, 1861.

Bateson, Mary, ed. *A Narrative of the Changes in the Ministry 1765-
1767.* London: Longmans, Green, 1898.

Beer, George Louis. *British Colonial Policy, 1754-1765.* New York:
Macmillan, 1907.

The Bowdoin and Temple Papers, Massachusetts Historical Society,
6th ser., vol. 9. Boston: The Society, 1897.

Bradford, Alden, ed. *Speeches of the Governors of Massachusetts
from 1765 to 1775.* Boston: Printed by Russell and Gardner, 1818.

Bullion, John L. *A Great and Necessary Measure: George Grenville
and the Genesis of the Stamp Act.* Columbia: University of Missouri Press, 1982.

Burke, Edmund. *Observations on a Late State of the Nation.* London: J. Dodsley, 1769.

———. *Speech of Edmund Burke, Esq. on American Taxation, April 19, 1774.* London: J. Dodsley, 1775.

Butterfield, L. H., ed. *The Adams Papers, Diary and Autobiography of John Adams,* vol. 2, 1771–1781. Cambridge, MA: Harvard University Press, 1961.

Cannan, Edwin, ed. [Adam Smith] *The Wealth of Nations, with an introduction and notes.* London: Methuen, 1904.

Cavendish, Sir Henry. *Debates of the House of commons, during the thirteenth Parliament of Great Britain, commonly called the unreported Parliament,* vol. 1. London: Longman, Orme, Brown, & Green, 1841.

Chandler, Thomas Bradbury. *A Friendly Address to all Reasonable Americans on the Subject of our Political Confusions; in which the Necessary Consequences of violently opposing the King's Troops, and of a General Non-importation are Fairly Stated.* America [New York]: Printed [by James Rivington] for the purchasers, 1774.

Channing, Edward. *The American Revolution, 1761-1789, A History of the United States,* vol. 3. New York: Macmillan, 1912.

Christie, Ian R. "A Vision of Empire: Thomas Whately and the Regulations Lately Made concerning the Colonies," *English Historical Review* 113, no. 451. 1998.

Cobbett's Parliamentary History of England, from the Norman Conquest, in 1066, to the Year 1803, AD 1722–1733, vol. 8. London: Printed by T. C. Hansard, 1811.

The Colden Letter Books, vol. 2. 1765–1775, Collections of the New York Historical Society, vol. 10. New York: Printed for the Society, 1877.

Commerce of Rhode Island, 1726-1800, Collections of the Massachusetts Historical Society, Seventh ser., vol. 9. Boston: The Society, 1914.

Connecticut General Assembly, *The Public Records of the Colony of Connecticut [1636-1776],* vol. 9. Hartford, CT: Press of the Case, 1890.

Copeland, Thomas W., ed. *The Correspondence of Edmund Burke,* vol. 1. Cambridge, UK: University Press, 1958.

Cushing, Harry Alonzo, ed. *The Writings of Samuel Adams, 1764-1769*, vol. 1. New York: G. P. Putnam's Sons, 1904.

Dexter, Franklin B., ed. "A Selection from The Correspondence and Miscellaneous Papers of Jared Ingersoll," *Papers of the New Haven Colony Historical Society*, vol. 9. New Haven, CT: The Society, 1918.

Dickerson, Oliver M. *The Navigation Acts and the American Revolution*. Philadelphia: University of Pennsylvania Press, 1951.

Dickinson, John. *Letters from a Farmer in Pennsylvania, to the Inhabitants of the British Colonies*. Philadelphia: Printed by David Hall, 1768.

Dulany, Daniel. *Considerations on the Propriety of Imposing Taxes in the British Colonies, for the Purpose of Raising a Revenue, by Act of Parliament*. North America: Printed by a North American, 1765.

Ellis, Joseph J. *The Cause: The American Revolution and Its Discontents, 1773-1783*. New York: Liveright, 2021.

Elofson, Warren M. *The Rockingham Connection and the Second Founding of the Whig Party 1768-1773*. Montreal: McGill-Queens's University Press, 1996.

The Fitch Papers, Volume II: January 1759-May 1766, Collections of the Connecticut Historical Society, vol. 18. Hartford, CT: The Society, 1920.

Ford, Paul Leicester, ed. *The Writings of John Dickinson, vol. 1, Political Writings: 1764-1774*. Philadelphia: Historical Society of Pennsylvania, 1895.

Ford, Worthington Chauncey, ed. *Journals of the Continental Congress, 1774-1789*, vol. 1, 1774. Washington: Government Printing Office, 1904.

Fortescue, John, ed. *The Correspondence of King George the Third from 1760 to December 1783*, vol. 1. London: Macmillan, 1927.

Gipson, Lawrence Henry. *Jared Ingersoll: a Study of American Loyalism in Relation to British Colonial Government*. New Haven, CT: Yale University Press, 1920.

Goebel, Dorothy Burne. "The 'New England Trade' and the French West Indies, 1763-1774: A Study in Trade Policies," *WMQ*, vol. 20, no. 3. July 1963.

Great Britain. Parliament. House of Commons. *Journals of the House of Commons*, vol. 30. London: H.M. Stationery Off., 1803.

Greene, Jack P., ed. *Great Britain and the American Colonies, 1606-1763*. Columbia: University of South Carolina Press, 1970.

Harper, Lawrence A. "The Effect of the Navigation Acts on the Thirteen Colonies." See Richard B. Morris.

Headlam, Cecil and Arthur Percival Newton, eds. *Calendar of State Papers: Colonial Series, America and West Indies*, vol. 37, 1730. London: His Majesty's Stationery Office, 1937.

———. *Calendar of State Papers: Colonial Series, America and West Indies*, vol. 39, 1732. London: His Majesty's Stationery Office, 1939.

———. *Calendar of State Papers: Colonial Series, America and West Indies*, vol. 40, 1733. London: His Majesty's Stationery Office, 1939.

Hutchinson, Thomas. *Strictures upon the Declaration of the Congress at Philadelphia: In a Letter to a Noble Lord, &c.* London, 1776.

———. *The History of the Province of Massachusetts Bay: from 1749 to 1774*, vol. 3. London: John Murray, 1828.

Jasper Mauduit: Agent in London for the Province of the Massachusetts-Bay 1762–1765, Massachusetts Historical Society Collections, vol. 74. Boston: The Society, 1918.

Jensen, Merrill, ed. *American Colonial Documents to 1776, English Historical Documents*, vol. 9. London: Eyre & Spottiswoode, 1955.

———. Commentary in, *Political Ideas of the American Revolution*, 3rd ed. New York: Barnes & Noble, 1958. First edition 1922.

———. *Tracts of the American Revolution, 1763-1776*. Indianapolis, IN: Bobbs-Merrill, 1966.

———. *The Founding of a Nation: A History of the American Revolution, 1763-1775*. New York: Oxford University Press, 1968.

Johnson, Allen S. "The Passage of the Sugar Act," *WMQ* 16, no. 4. 1959.

Journal of the Votes and Proceedings of the General Assembly of the Colony of New-York, vol. 2. New York: Published by Order of the General Assembly, 1766.

Journals of the House of Representatives of Massachusetts: 1763-1764, vol. 40. Boston: Massachusetts Historical Society, 1970.

Journals of the House of Representatives of Massachusetts: 1764-1765, vol. 41. Boston: Massachusetts Historical Society, 1971.

Jucker, Ninetta S., ed. *The Jenkinson Papers, 1760-1766*. London: Macmillan, 1949.

Kamensky, Jane. *A Revolution in Color: The World of John Singleton Copley*. New York: W. W. Norton, 2016.

Keppel, George Thomas, Earl of Albemarle, ed., *Memoirs of the Marquis of Rockingham and his contemporaries: With original letters and documents now first published*, vol. 1. London: Richard Bentley, 1852.

Kimball, Gertrude S., ed. *The Correspondence of the Colonial Governors of Rhode Island 1723-1775*, vol. 1. New York: Houghton, Mifflin, 1902.

Knollenberg, Bernard. *Origin of the American Revolution: 1759–1766*. New York: Macmillan, 1960.

———. *Growth of the American Revolution: 1766-1775*. Indianapolis, IN: Liberty Fund, 2003, originally published 1975.

Knox, William. *The Present State of the Nation: Particularly with Respect to its Trade, Finances, etc. etc. Addressed To The King And Both Houses Of Parliament*. Dublin: Printed for W. Watson, 1768.

———. *The Controversy Between Great Britain and Her Colonies Reviewed*. London: printed for J. Almon, 1769.

Labaree, Leonard W., ed. *The Papers of Benjamin Franklin*, vol. 10. New Haven, CT: Yale University Press, 1966.

———. *The Papers of Benjamin Franklin*, vol. 11. New Haven, CT: Yale University Press, 1967.

———. *The Papers of Benjamin Franklin*, vol. 13. New Haven, CT: Yale University Press, 1969.

———. *The Papers of Benjamin Franklin*, vol. 14. New Haven, CT: Yale University Press, 1970.

Langford, Paul. *The First Rockingham Administration: 1765-1766*. London: Oxford University Press, 1973.

Langford, Paul, ed. *The Writings and Speeches of Edmund Burke, Party, Parliament, and the American Crisis 1766-1774*, vol. 2. Oxford, UK: Clarendon Press, 1981.

Lind, John. *Remarks on the Principal Acts of the Thirteenth Parliament of Great Britain.* London: Printed for T. Payne, 1775.

Marshall, P. J. *Edmund Burke and the British Empire in the West Indies: Wealth, Power, and Slavery.* Oxford, UK: Oxford University Press, 2019.

Martin, Alfred S. "The King's Customs: Philadelphia, 1763-1774." *WMQ* 5, no. 2. 1948.

Massachusetts Historical Society. *Proceedings of the Massachusetts Historical Society*, vol. 13. Boston: Massachusetts Historical Society, 1875.

———. *Proceedings of the Massachusetts Historical Society*, vol. 20. Boston: Massachusetts Historical Society, 1884.

———. "The Trumbull Papers," *Collections of the Massachusetts Historical Society*, 5th ser., vol. 9. Boston: The Society, 1885.

———. "London Merchants on the Stamp Act Repeal," *Proceedings of the Massachusetts Historical Society*, Third ser., vol. 55. Boston: The Society, 1923.

Matthews, Albert, ed. *Letters of Dennys De Berdt 1757-1770.* Cambridge, MA: Wilson and Son, 1911.

McCusker, John and Russell Menard. *The Economy of British America, 1607-1786.* Chapel Hill: University of North Carolina Press, 1985.

Morgan, Edmund S. "Colonial Ideas of Parliamentary Power 1764-1766," *WMQ* 5, no. 3. 1948.

———. "The Postponement of the Stamp Act," *WMQ* 7, no. 3. 1950.

———. *Prologue to Revolution: Sources and Documents on the Stamp Act Crisis, 1764-1766.* Chapel Hill: University of North Carolina Press, 1959.

Morgan, Edmund S. & Helen M. Morgan. *The Stamp Act Crisis: Prologue to Revolution.* Chapel Hill: University of North Carolina Press, 1953.

Morison, Samuel Eliot, ed. *Sources & Documents Illustrating the American Revolution: 1764-1788*, Second edition. London: Oxford University Press, 1929. First Published 1923.

Morris, Richard B. ed. *The Era of the American Revolution.* New York: Columbia University Press, 1939.

Munro, James, ed. *Acts of the Privy Council of England: Colonial Series, AD 1745-1766*, vol. 4. London, 1911.

Namier, Sir Lewis and John Brooke. *The House of Commons, 1754-1790*, vol. 2. London: Her Majesty's Stationary Office, 1964.

———. *Charles Townshend*. London: Macmillan, 1964.

Nelson, Eric. *The Royalist Revolution: Monarchy and the American Founding*. Cambridge, MA: Harvard University Press, 2014.

Nelson, William, ed. *New Jersey Archives: Newspaper Abstracts*, vol. 5: 1762-1765. Paterson, NJ: Call Printing and Publishing, 1902.

Nicolson, Colin, ed. *The Papers of Francis Bernard: Governor of Colonial Massachusetts, 1760-1769, Volume 1: 1759-1763*, The Colonial Society of Massachusetts, vol. 73. Boston: Colonial Society of Massachusetts, 2007.

———. *The Papers of Francis Bernard: Governor of Colonial Massachusetts, 1760–1769, Volume 2: 1764–1765, The Colonial Society of Massachusetts*, vol. 81. Boston: Colonial Society of Massachusetts, 2012.

———. *The Papers of Francis Bernard: Governor of Colonial Massachusetts, 1760-1769, Volume 3: 1766-1767, Publications of the Colonial Society of Massachusetts*, vol. 83. Boston: Colonial Society of Massachusetts, 2013.

———. *The Papers of Francis Bernard: Governor of Colonial Massachusetts, 1760-1769, Volume 4: 1768*, Publications of the Colonial Society of Massachusetts, vol. 86. Boston: Colonial Society of Massachusetts, 2015.

Observations on several acts of Parliament, passed in the 4th, 6th and 7th years of His present Majesty's reign: and also, on the conduct of the officers of the customs, since those acts were passed, and the Board of Commissioners appointed to reside in America. Published by the merchants of Boston. Boston: Printed by Edes & Gill, 1769.

Otis, James. *The Rights of the British Colonies Asserted and Proved*. Boston, 1764.

The Parliamentary History of England, From the Earliest Period to the Year 1803, vol. 15. A. D. 1753-1765. London: Printed by T.C. Hansard, 1813.

The Parliamentary History of England, From the Earliest Period to the Year 1803, vol. 16. A. D. 1765-1771. London: Printed by T.C. Hansard, 1813.

Peterson, Merrill D., comp. *Thomas Jefferson: Writings*. New York: Library of America, 1984.

Pickering, Danby. *The Statutes at Large, from Magna Charta to the end of the Eleventh Parliament of Great Britain, Anno 1761*, vol. 25. Cambridge, UK: Printed by Joseph Bentham, 1763.

———. *The Statutes at Large, from Magna Charta to the end of the Eleventh Parliament of Great Britain, Anno 1761*, vol. 26. Cambridge, UK: Printed by Joseph Bentham, 1764.

———. *The Statutes at Large, from the Second to the 9th year of King George II*, vol. 16. Cambridge, UK: Printed by Joseph Bentham, 1765.

———. *The Statutes at Large, from Magna Charta to the end of the Eleventh Parliament of Great Britain, Anno 1761*, vol. 27. Cambridge, UK: Printed by John Archdeacon, 1767.

Pitman, Frank Wesley. *The Development of the British West Indies, 1700-1763*. New Haven, CT: Yale University Press, 1917.

The Political State of Great Britain. Containing The Months of July, August, September, October, November, and December. 1731, vol. 42. London: Printed for the Executors of Mr. Boyer, 1731.

Pownall, Thomas. *The Administration of the British Colonies*. Fifth edition, vol. 1. London: Printed for J. Walter, 1774.

Price, Richard. *Observations on the Nature of Civil Liberty, the Principles of Government, and the Justice and Policy of the War with America*. London: Printed for T. Cadell, 1776.

Rabushka, Alvin. *Taxation in Colonial America*. Princeton, NJ: Princeton University Press, 2008.

Reasons against the renewal of the Sugar Act as it will be prejudicial to the trade, not only of the northern colonies, but to that of Great-Britain also. Boston: Province of the Massachusetts-Bay, 1764.

Reid, John Phillip. *The Authority to Tax, Constitutional History of the American Revolution*, vol. 2. Madison: University of Wisconsin Press, 1987.

———. *The Authority to Legislate, Constitutional History of the American Revolution*, vol. 3. Madison: University of Wisconsin Press, 1991.

———. *Constitutional History of the American Revolution* Abridged Edition. Madison: University of Wisconsin Press, 1995.

A Report of the Record Commissioners of the City of Boston, Containing the Boston Town Records, 1758 to 1769. Boston, 1886.

Ricord, Frederick W. and Wm. Nelson, eds. *Documents Relating to the Colonial History of the State of New Jersey 1757-1767*, First ser., vol. 9. Newark, NJ: Daily Advertiser Printing House, 1885.

Schlesinger, Arthur M. *The Colonial Merchants and the American Revolution, 1763-1766.* New York: Columbia University, 1918.

Sheridan, Richard B. "The Molasses Act and the Market Strategy of the British Sugar Planters," *Journal of Economic History 17*, no. 1. 1957.

Shumate, Ken. *1764: The First Year of the American Revolution.* Yardley, PA: Westholme Publishing, 2021.

———. "The Sugar Act: A Brief History," *Journal of the American Revolution,* September 17, 2018.

———. "The Exception to 'no taxation without representation,'" *JAR,* September 9, 2019.

———. "The Molasses Act: A Brief History," *JAR: Annual Volume 2020.* Yardley, PA: Westholme Publishing, 2020.

———. "Reasons against the Renewal of the Sugar Act," *JAR,* June 4, 11, and 18, 2020.

———. "Observations on Several Acts of Parliament," *JAR,* June 9, 2021.

Simmons, R. C. and P. D. G. Thomas, eds. *Proceedings and Debates of the British Parliaments Respecting North America, 1754-1783,* vol. 1, *1754-1764.* Millwood, NY: Kraus International, 1982.

———. *Proceedings and Debates of the British Parliaments Respecting North America, 1754-1783,* vol. 2, *1765-1768.* Millwood, NY: Kraus International, 1983.

Smith, Adam. *An Inquiry into the Nature and Causes of the Wealth of Nations,* vol. 2. London: Printed for W. Strahan and T. Cadell, fifth edition, 1789; first edition 1776.

Smith, Paul Hubert, ed. *Letters of Delegates to Congress, 1774-1789,* vol. 1, *August 1774-August 1775.* Washington: Library of Congress, 1976.

Smith, William James, ed. *The Grenville papers: being the correspondence of Richard Grenville, earl Temple, K.G., and the right Hon.George Grenville, their friends and contemporaries*, vol. 3. London: John Murray, 1853.

Sosin, Jack M. *Agents and Merchants: British Colonial Policy and the Origins of the American Revolution, 1763-1775*. Lincoln: University of Nebraska Press, 1965.

Southwick, Albert B. "The Molasses Act—Source of Precedents," *WMQ* 8, no. 3. 1951.

Sutherland, Lucy S. "Edmund Burke and the First Rockingham Ministry," *EHR* 47, no. 185. 1932.

Taylor, Robert J. "Israel Mauduit," *New England Quarterly* 24, no. 2. 1951.

Taylor, W. S. and J. H. Pringle, eds. *Correspondence of William Pitt, Earl of Chatham*, vol. 3. London: John Murray, 1839.

Thacher, Oxenbridge. *The Sentiments of a British American*. Boston: Edes & Gill, 1764.

Thomas, P. D. G. *British Politics and the Stamp Act Crisis: The First Phase of the American Revolution, 1763-1767*. Oxford, UK: Clarendon Press, 1975.

———. "George III and the American Revolution," *History* 70, no. 228, 1985.

———. *The Townshend Duties Crisis: The Second Phase of the American Revolution, 1767-1773*. Oxford, UK: Clarendon Press, 1987.

———. *Revolution in America: Britain and the Colonies, 1763–1776*. Cardiff: University of Wales Press, 1992.

Thomas, P. D. G., ed. "Parliamentary Diaries of Nathaniel Ryder. 1764–7," *Camden Miscellany*, vol. 23, Camden Society, 4th ser., vol. 7. London: Royal Historical Society, 1969.

Tyler, John W. and Elizabeth Dubrulle, eds. *The Correspondence of Thomas Hutchinson, Volume 1: 1740-1766*. The Colonial Society of Massachusetts, vol. 84. Boston: Colonial Society of Massachusetts, 2014.

Ubbelohde, Carl. *The Vice-Admiralty Courts and the American Revolution*. Chapel Hill: University of North Carolina Press, 1960.

Walmsley, Andrew Stephen. *Thomas Hutchinson and the Origins of the American Revolution.* New York: New York University Press, 1999.

Watson, D. H. "Joseph Harrison and the Liberty Incident," *WMQ* 20, no. 4. 1963.

Whately, Thomas. *The Regulations Lately Made Concerning the Colonies, and the Taxes Imposed Upon Them, Considered.* London: Printed for J. Wilkie, 1765.

Willcox, William B., ed. *The Papers of Benjamin Franklin*, vol. 16. New Haven, CT: Yale University Press, 1972.

Wood, Gordon S. *The American Revolution: A History.* New York: Modern Library, 2002.

———. *Power and Liberty: Constitutionalism in the American Revolution.* New York: Oxford University Press, 2021.

Wood, Gordon S., ed. *The American Revolution: Writings from the Pamphlet Debate 1764–1776*, vol. 1. New York: Library of America, 2015.

———. *The American Revolution: Writings from the Pamphlet Debate 1764–1776*, vol. 2. New York: Library of America, 2015.

INDEX

Adams, John, x-xi, 9, 18, 96, 161
Adams, Samuel, 88, 111
Address of Assembly of Barbados to the King, 12-13
Address to the People of Great Britain, 58
The Administration of the British Colonies (Pownall), 134
Admiralty Courts, 10, 49, 70-71, 73-75, 77, 85, 96, 98, 107, 117, 133
Africa, 32, 35, 46, 118, 156
American Committee, 104, 118-119, 121
Azores, 52, 55

Bailyn, Bernard, 39, 82, 84
Barclay & Sons, 66
Barnard, John, xviii, 4, 6, 18
Barrington, Lord, 145, 149
Bay of Biscay, 127
Beckford, William, 45, 95, 119
Benevolus (Franklin), 139, 141
Bernard, Francis, 23-24, 27, 72, 90, 134, 145-146, 148-150
Board of Customs, 22
Board of Trade, xiv, xviii, 14, 24, 72, 90, 132, 135
Bollan, William, 103
Boston Evening Post, 159
Boston Gazette, 96, 108-109, 130
Boston Tea Party, 160
boycott, 149, 152, 154, 159
British Plantations, 59, 63, 121, 126, 133

Burke, Edmund, viii, 13, 43-44, 67-68, 77, 82, 97, 106, 119, 131, 151

Cape Finisterre, 124, 127-129
Charles II, 123
Chatham, Lord, 131, 135, 140
cockets, 65-68
coffee, 53, 55-56, 63, 123-124, 137, 162
Collectors, importance of, 27, 60
Connecticut protest, 36, 87
Continental Congress, viii, xi, 18, 43, 58, 71, 78, 96, 111, 115, 122, 152, 160, 162
The Controversy Between Great Britain and Her Colonies Reviewed (Knox), 147
Cruger, Jr., Henry, 103, 106
Currency Act, 78, 141
Cushing, Thomas, 25, 37-38, 88

Dartmouth, Earl of, 103, 105
De Berdt, Dennys, 101, 106-107, 134-135, 153, 155, 158
Declaration of Independence, 90
Declaratory Act, 107, 110-111, 135, 143, 153, 158
Dickinson, John, 1, 144-145, 147, 159
Dowdeswell, William, 119, 151-153
Duane, James, 161
Dunbar, Mr., xiv-xv, xvii, 3, 15

Ellis, Joseph, x

An Essay on the Trade of the Northern Colonies of Great Britain in North America, An, (Hopkins), 34
external taxes, 26-27, 79-82, 86, 95-96, 120, 139-147, 152-153, 161

Farmer's Letters (Dickinson), 144-147
Fitch, Thomas, 87-88, 95
Franklin, Benjamin, 26, 28, 64, 79-82, 88, 91, 104, 139, 141-142, 155, 158
Free Port Act, 122
Fuller, Rose, 104, 121

Galloway, Joseph, 142
George II, 7, 13, 25, 27, 36-37, 157-158
George III, 93, 94, 115, 158, 162
George III, 19, 53, 64, 67, 72, 78, 83, 93-94, 99, 107, 115, 122, 127, 129, 143, 154-155, 157-158, 162
Grenville, George, 17-22, 24, 26, 37, 43-50, 57, 67-69, 78-79, 84, 94-95, 99-101, 109, 112, 119, 135, 142

Hancock, John, 109, 130, 144
Harrison, Joseph, 94-95, 146-147
Hopkins, Stephen, 33, 35-36
Hopkinson, Francis, 27
House of Commons, viii, xiv, xvi, xviii-xix, 4-6, 13, 15-15, 18, 30, 36-38, 43-44, 48-49, 79, 82, 86, 89-90, 95, 100, 102, 104-105, 108, 117-119, 128, 132, 134-135, 141, 143, 151, 153-154, 158
House of Lords, xviii-xix, 6-7, 108, 128
Hovering Act, 19, 24-25, 63, 72
Huske, John, 48, 141

Hutchinson, Thomas, 23, 89, 103

Ingersoll, Jared, 92, 95
internal taxes, 26-27, 78-82, 85-88, 91, 95-96, 99, 139-143, 145-147, 152-153, 161
Ireland, xiii-xiv, xvii, 10, 64, 127, 129

Jackson, Richard, 23, 26-28, 64, 88, 91
Jamaica, 104
Jefferson, Thomas, 127
Jenkinson, Charles, 18-19, 22, 48, 76
Jensen, Merrill, xi
Johnson, William Samuel, 140, 143

King's Arms Tavern, 118-119
Knox, William, 112, 147

Leonard, Daniel, 96
Letters from a Farmer in Pennsylvania (Dickinson), 144-147
Liberty, 144
Lind, John, 13
London Chronicle, 141
London Gazette, 108

Madeira, 46-47, 52, 55, 137
Magna Charta, 81
Massachuset's Bay, 90
Massachusetts Gazette, 96
Massachusetts General Assembly, 89
Massachusetts General Court, 29, 33
Massachusetts protest, 29, 88
Mauduit, Israel, 37
Mauduit, Jasper, 25, 29, 37-38, 79, 89
A Memorial to the Lords Commissioners of His Majesty's Treasury, 37
Moffett, Thomas, 109

molasses, vii-viii, x-xi, xiii-xiv, xvi-xix, 3-5, 7, 9, 11, 13-14, 19-23, 26-27, 30-32, 34-36, 43, 46-49, 52, 56-57, 59-62, 85, 90-93, 98, 107, 117-121, 123, 125-126, 131, 136-139, 147, 152, 156-157, 159-160, 162
Molosses Act, 23, *see also* Sugar Act of 1733

Navigation Acts, xvi, 17, 20, 45, 50-51, 63, 85, 100, 136
Newcastle, Duke of, 6, 121
Newport Mercury, 22
New York Gazette, 22
New York General Assembly, 36
New York protest, 36, 86
North, Lord, 158-159

Observations on Several Acts of Parliament, 155
On the Propriety of Taxing America, 141
Otis, James, 38, 88, 134

Partridge, Richard, xix, 5-7
Pennsylvania Chronicle, 144
Pennsylvania committee of correspondence, 26
Pennsylvania Gazette, 78
Pennsylvania protest, 91
Pitkin, William, 140, 143
Pitt, William, 1st Earl of Chatham, 15, 131, 135, 140
Plantation Act of 1673, xv, 5, 57, 64
Portugal, 12, 24, 34, 46, 55
Pownall, Thomas, 134, 158
Price, Richard, 38
Privy Council, 19-21
Providence Gazette, 33

Reasons Against the Renewal of the Sugar Act, 33

Regulations Lately Made (Whately), 50
Remarks on the Trade of the Colony, 36
Rhode Island protest, 33, 35, 91
Roberts, Hugh, 104
Rockingham, Lord, 44, 95, 99-103, 105, 107-109, 112, 117-119, 122, 130-131, 147, 152
Royal Navy, 15, 19, 21, 63
rum, vii, x-xi, xiii-xix, 3-5, 7-8, 11, 14, 19, 22, 24-27, 30, 32, 34-35, 37, 47-48, 52, 56-57, 59-60, 85, 93, 118, 132-133, 156

Savile, George, 103, 105
Seven Years' War, x, 14-15, 17
Shelburne, Lord, 132, 134-135, 148-149
Sherwood, Joseph, 121
A Short Account of a Late Short Administration (Burke), 131
Smith, William, 107
smuggling, 14-15, 17, 19, 27, 46-49, 51, 59, 61, 66, 69, 76, 92, 125, 133
Society for Encouraging Trade and Commerce, 29
Spain, 12, 24, 34, 46, 127-128
Speech on American Taxation (Burke), 82, 151-152
Stamp Act, vii, x, 45, 48, 93-94, 96-112, 117-118, 131, 134-135, 145, 149, 151, 153
State of the Trade, 33
Sugar Act of 1733
    George II and, 7, 13, 25, 27, 36-37
    how the act came about and, 4-7
    illicit trade during the war and, 14-16
    lack of enforcement and, 13-14
    Molasses Act and, 23
    nature of the act and, 13

proof of innocence and, 11-12
protests against and, 29-39
text of the act and, 7-13
Sugar Act of 1764
committee of ways and means,
45-48
George III and, 53, 64, 67, 83,
107, 115, 158
justification of, 50-53
most oppressive provisions of, 77
origins of, 44-45
overview of, 43-44
passage of the act and, 49-50
protection for customs officers
and, 73-76
protests against and, 85-97
seizure of ships and cargo, 71-72
text of the act and, 53-77
Sugar Act of 1766
accepting taxation and, 136
commercial problems and, 132-
135
complexity of the regulations and,
128-129
end of a ministry and, 130-131
George III and, 122
news to America and, 129-130
nonimportation resolutions and,
144, 149-150, 154-155, 159
nonimportation resolutions and,
149-150
overview of, 117-118
protest to the Townshend duties
and, 148
response to Sugar Act duties and,
132
revenue and, 136-138
revisions to, 156-157
Speech on American taxation
(Burke), 151-152
text of, 122-128
Sugar Bill of 1731, xiii, xvi, xix
Sugar Bill of 1732, xviii-xix
*Summary View of the Rights of
British America* (Jefferson),
127-128

Tea-Duty Bill, 158
Temple, John, 92, 94-95, 140, 142
Thacher, Oxenbridge, 71, 88
Thomson, Charles, 104
Townshend, Charles, vii, 99, 139-
141, 143-144, 148-149,
151-155, 158
Townshend Revenue Act
American reaction to, 151-152
call for repeal and, 158
nonimportant resolutions and,
144, 149-150, 154-155, 159
origins of, 143
Trecothick, Barlow, 100-102, 106
Tyton, John, 22

Ubbelohde, Carl, historian, 74

Vice admiralty, 71, 74, 92

West India Island Committee, 104,
118-119
West Indies, xi, xiii-xvi, 3, 5, 12-14,
17-21, 24, 31-32, 34, 45-46,
51-52, 54, 61, 63, 79, 93,
104, 120, 122, 125
Whately, Thomas, 38, 50, 54, 56-
59, 61-64, 66-69, 76-77, 92,
95, 140, 142
White, Samuel, 101, 106
Winnington, Thomas, 6
Wood, Gordon, historian, 85
Wood, William, 22

Yeates, Robert, 22
Yorke, Charles, 108